How to Sell My Products

Published by
Lotus Press

How to Sell My Products

Michael E. Allen

Lotus
PRESS
4263/3, Ansari Road,
Darya Ganj, New Delhi-110002

Lotus Press
4263/3, Ansari Road, Darya Ganj, New Delhi-110002
Ph.: 32903912, 23280047, E-mail: lotus_press@sify.com
www.lotuspress.co.in

HOW TO SELL MY PRODUCTS

ISBN: 81-8382-021-2

Reprint: 2009

Published by: Lotus Press, New Delhi-110 002.
Printed at: Arpit Printer, Delhi

PREFACE

Sales is one of the major aspect of product management. It involves most or many of the following activities, including cultivating prospective buyers in a market segment; conveying the features, advantages and benefits of a product or service to the lead; and closing the sale or coming to agreement on pricing and services.

For many people, one of the most daunting aspects of running a business is trying to sell your product or service to someone. The thought of attempting to persuade someone to buy something in which you have invested so much time and effort can bring out even the most determined entrepreneur in a cold sweat.

This book provides succinct guidelines, useful tips and thought provoking ideas to sell your product successfully. The lessons are easy to learn and they will help you forge more rewarding customer relationships, a higher income, and a richer career satisfaction. This book is a must-read for any salesperson who wants to improve and reach the next level of success.

Editor

For many people, one of the most daunting aspects of running a business is trying to sell your product or service to someone. The thought of attempting to persuade someone to buy something in which you have invested so much time and effort can bring out even the most determined entrepreneur in a cold sweat.

This action-oriented book provides succinct guidelines, useful tips and thought provoking ideas to sell your product successfully. The lessons are easy to learn and they will help you forge more rewarding customer relationships, a higher income, and a richer career satisfaction. This book is a must-read for any salesperson who wants to improve and reach the next level of success.

For many people one of the most daunting aspects of running a business is trying to sell your product or service to someone. The thought of attempting to persuade someone to buy something in which you have invested so much time and effort yet being met with [illegible] for a salesperson.

This user-friendly book provides many strategies, techniques and thought-provoking ideas to help you promote successfully. The lessons are easy to read and they will help you forge more rewarding customer relationships, a higher income, and a greater career satisfaction. This book is a must read for any salesperson who wants to improve and reach the next level of success.

CONTENTS

1

HOW TO SELL MY PRODUCT EFFECTIVELY

Sale is a type of contract for the exchange of goods, property or services. It involves activities including cultivating prospective buyers or leads in a market segment; conveying the features, advantages and benefits of a product or service to the lead; and closing the sale or coming to agreement on pricing and services.

1.1. BASIC STEPS IN A SALES PROCESS

The basics of the actual sales process, and customising them for your business, are critical in building customer relationships. Whatever your setting, and whether you sell a product or service, the following steps are the ones you should use.

1. *Know your product or service.* Before you even have a preliminary conversation with a prospect, it is essential that you clearly understand what attributes make your product or service unique or desirable, and why people should want what you have to offer,
2. *Make initial contact.* The actual sales conversations with people in your target market begin when you start letting them get to know you, and vice-versa.

3. *Exchange information.* This step consists of meeting with your prospects, asking them questions, uncovering their needs, giving them information about your product or service, and determining how it might fill those stated needs. Don't be afraid to acknowledge gaps in your knowledge or understanding; such sincerity comes through in a positive way.
4. *Propose a solution.* Once you have ascertained that there is a good fit between you and the prospect, you can propose how your product or service would specifically solve a problem or handle a need. By understanding the features and benefits of competing products or services, you can also prove at this point how what you offer is better.
5. *Confirm the sale.* Rather than focusing on "closing the sale," a term that indicates the end of the process, confirming the sale means you are reviewing the customer's willingness and ability to make a commitment. It is a natural extension of a sales relationship built on a foundation of trust, respect and rapport.
6. *Deliver.* Although actually delivering your product or service is not technically part of the sales process, it is a very critical step. If you don't deliver, you don't have a sale. In addition, during this step you have an excellent opportunity to continue to build trust and cement your relationship with your client.
7. *Follow up.* This is the time to find out how your client likes your product or service. This stage provides an ideal chance to create repeat business or get referrals to new prospects. And if there is a problem, you have an opportunity to correct it.

1.2. USEFUL SALES TECHNIQUES

Although selling by rote formula is no longer appropriate in today's environment, some simple techniques can be very effective when properly applied in the context of creating business relationships. You can focus on building trust all day, but if you don't ask for what you want, you still won't make the sale. For example, you might have made a good convection with a fellow industry organisation member, but there will be no possibility of a sale unless you spend some time discussing how the two of you might have a match. In a retail environment, it could be as simple as introducing yourself to customers, rather than staying behind the counter and ignoring their presence.

Another traditional technique is understanding and using body language. Knowing how to interpret prospects' folded arms or eye contact could give you much-needed information about how comfortable they are with you, or how ready they are to make a purchase decision. Also, when you know how to use body language appropriately, you can communicate your interest, concern or enthusiasm without words. It is well known that communication is 50 percent body language, 40 percent tone of voice, and 10 percent the actual words used.

1.2.1. Relationship Selling

Many small business people have great ideas for products or services, but don't want to sell or don't know how. They've defined their target market and how to reach it, and have mastered the financial aspects of running a company. However, often missing is a clear understanding of the sales process or the willingness and ability to initiate successful sales conversations, and not get stopped by people saying "no."

What is it about selling that makes so many entrepreneurs shudder, especially those who are the sole salesperson for their firm? Very often they are affected by preconceived notions as to what selling is. Or they have a strong fear of rejection — when a prospect says "no," they take it personally. Letting these negative ideas get in the way of selling is one way to ensure your venture will fail. After all, if you don't make sales, you don't have a business, no matter how good a product you have, or how well you've done your marketing.

There is a way to sell that is positive, rewarding and enjoyable. And it helps handle that fear of rejection as well. It's called relationship selling, and is the way effective, professional sales people have always operated. Relationship selling applies to any kind of business, whether retail or business-to-business, product or service. While the steps to the sales process may vary slightly for each type, the overall theme of building relationships is consistent throughout.

Although a lot has been written recently about relationship selling, the concept itself is not new. The principles involved have always worked, and are even more important in today's highly service-oriented market environment. Relationship selling does not consist of a simple set of techniques you have to master. It is a way of conducting yourself in the business world that is flexible, cooperative and professional. When selling in a context of building healthy relationships, you are operating as an ethical, considerate and helpful human being. You are also building your communication and other personal development skills. This is not only satisfying, but also quite effective in creating a steady stream of sales for your business.

Relationship selling applies to any kind of business, whether retail or business-to-business, product or service. While the steps to the sales process may vary slightly for each type, the overall theme of building relationships is consistent throughout.

Relationship selling is a win/win game. If the product or service being sold truly meets the needs of the buyer, both parties benefit as a result of the sale. Today's customers have become more sophisticated and demanding of higher levels of customer service than ever before. They want someone they can trust who understands their needs and wants. This is particularly important during slow economic times, when most people make buying decisions, even small ones, very carefully.

The best sources of new business are existing customers and referrals from these customers. To help ensure the success of your venture, take the time to build relationships with your customers, rather than just focusing on making the immediate sale. Although relationship selling may take longer to produce results, it is definitely worth it in the long run. You will be well rewarded with high levels of repeat business and referrals from happy customers.

1.2.2. Fulfilling Customers' Needs

The better your product or service fits your customers' needs, the more sales you will have. When customers know you sincerely care about what they want and need, they will feel secure that they are making the right decision in buying from you. By clearly identifying the needs of your customers, you can also confirm whether or not they are part of your target market. Even if they really do not require what you have, you can still build trust and improve your relationship by being candid and referring them to a more suitable resource. You never know when this good deed will return to you in the form of highly qualified referral business.

1.2.3. Use of Open-Ended Questions

One of the best ways to obtain pertinent details about a customer's needs is to ask questions that elicit information, rather than a simple "yes" or "no." The classic interview questions are: who, what, when, where, why and how. For example, "who will be using this product?", or "when will you be ready to make a decision?". While you are asking, also respond at appropriate times by linking key product or service benefits with the prospect's stated requirements. The result is an interactive conversation where information is exchanged and both parties expand their knowledge.

Sometimes it might be appropriate to elicit certain specifics. For example, "how long have you been in business?" Don't be afraid to ask such closed-ended questions. They can be quite useful, even though they don't provide the in-depth information acquired from open-ended queries. Open and closed ended questions were often used in the outmoded formula style of selling, but with a more insidious goal of finding out enough information so the sale could be made whether or not it was beneficial to the customer. In contrast, as a sales professional focused on building relationships, you are operating in a context of integrity and trust with the goal of having customers for the long-term, not just for the moment.

1.2.4. Listening More

Something magical happens when people give their undivided attention to others, without interrupting or focusing on what they are going to say next. This is true whether the environment is professional or personal. However, it is often overlooked in the context of establishing a business relationship, much to the detriment of the seller. After all, if you do all the talking, you will never learn anything about your prospect. When you listen more than you talk, customers realise you are genuinely interested in them, and that you are trying to understand their specific situation. They feel more comfortable with you, and will soon realise you are on their side. Make active listening a regular practice, and you will find it much easier to create excellent relationships with your customers.

1.2.5. Dealing with Customer Rejections

One of the main reasons small business owners dislike selling is that they don't like to get rejected. This is a basic and very understandable human reaction. However, excluding financial considerations, people generally say "no" for one of three basic reasons: they don't like you, they don't trust you, or what you are offering is not what they want or need. Aside from the fact that not everybody will like you, if you have done your job, focused on building trust, and made sure that there is a fit between you and the prospect, you will rarely hear "no." At worst, the timing will not be quite right, or you may be referred to other people who might respond positively.

Many entrepreneurs have their survival directly linked with the success of their operation, which makes rejection very serious indeed. When starting out, make sure you have at least a 12-month cushion of money for living expenses while you are building your business. Then try focusing on the "numbers game" aspect of selling to put things in perspective. The truth is that you need to be engaged in a number of selling "conversations" at any one time in order to reach your desired goals. Not all of these conversations lead to immediate sales, and you will normally have to replace approximately 10 percent of your customer base every year, as people move, change jobs or go out of business. So make a game of it. While you are busy building relationships, make sure you are building enough of them. Focusing on the game aspect can help diminish your feelings of rejection every time someone says "no." You will be better able to move on to the next prospect, knowing you made your best effort.

1.2.6. Trust Building

People tend to do business with those they like and trust. Look into your own buying experiences. Have you ever walked away from a transaction because you did not trust the salesperson to deliver what was being promised, or because you just plain didn't like the man or woman? And conversely, haven't you found yourself going back again and again to do business with helpful and honest sales people?

How do you build trust in a business environment? Let your prospects and customers get to know you. Make sure they understand why you started your business, and why you believe in your product or service. You might also get involved in industry or neighbourhood organisations where you can meet your prospects and customers in a different environment. They can experience another side of you, and get to know you as a person, not just as a vendor. While you are still selling the benefits of your product or service, you are also selling yourself.

Another way to build trust is to keep your word. From follow-up calls to delivering on time, keeping your word can be one of your most powerful sales tools. Of course unexpected things do happen, and sometimes you cannot keep your promises. When this occurs, communicate with your prospect or customer, and inquire whether the change is workable and what you can do to lessen the inconvenience. That way, you keep your trust level intact, or may even strengthen it as a result.

1.2.7. When to Say "No"

Even after doing and saying all the right things, you may still get "no" for an answer. Sometimes this can provide an opportunity to redirect the sales situation or develop a new proposal. At other times, it just signals that it's best to move on to the next prospect.

Here's what top sales people suggest doing when the answer is absolutely, positively "no":

1. *Thank the prospect for the opportunity to bid for the business.* This basic precept is particularly valuable if you also ask the prospect for feedback. What factors contributed to the decision? What did your product or service lack? What did you do or not do that lost the sale?
2. *Determine whether to pursue the business further.* Research shows that successful sales people have more failed calls calls— that end with a "no" from the prospect — than mediocre sales people. Successful sales people know when to walk away. They've thoroughly explored the prospect's needs, and recognise that the product or service being offered does not meet them.
3. *Stay in touch.* If your analysis convinces you to pursue the business, stay in touch with the prospect. Send articles of interest, or invite the prospect to events that are particularly relevant. But avoid routine follow-up calls. Phone only when you have information that meets a specific need the prospect is trying to address but by the way they are in business.

Sales professionals:

1. Are committed to the success of their clients' businesses, as well as their own.
2. Have clearly stated business and life goals.
3. Take time to educate themselves, and are always open to learning how to improve their sales skills.
4. Spend spare time in sales-related activities, whether within their industry or contributing to other entrepreneurs.
5. Take personal responsibility for both their successes and failures, rather than blaming others for any setbacks.
6. Keep track of their progress, including accurate records of conversations with clients and appropriate follow-up times, as well as their level of activity during each step of the sales process.
7. Are determined and persistent, and don't let anything discourage or slow them down.

1.3. TIPS FOR SELLING MORE EFFECTIVELY

Do you want to sell more successfully using an honourable and straightforward approach? The following sales tips will help you be perceived as a trusted sales professional by buyers. Incorporating these sales tips into your selling process will differentiate you from the rest and help you sell more successfully.

1. *Attitude can be everything.* It is important to remember that your attitudes drive all actions and these actions are perceived by buyers as trust-building or trust-breaking. The most important change you can make to sell more successfully is to adopt and reinforce attitudes that will lead to actions resulting in greater levels of trust.

Conversely, it is just as important to "lose the attitudes" that result in actions that are trust-breaking.

2. *Truly believe in the product or service and company for which you sell.* This is a really difficult hurdle for most sellers who strongly believe in straightforward selling. If you don't believe your products or services will benefit your buyers, then you will constantly be in conflict with yourself during the sales process. If selling using a straightforward platform is truly important to you, it might be necessary for you to find another product or service you will better represent to truly be successful using this approach.
3. *Intimately know the product or service and environment in which you sell.* Do you need to be an expert? Maybe not. But it can only benefit your customer to know as much as possible so you can identify if your product or service can best meet their needs. A significant aspect of building trust with your buying counterparts is quickly establishing credibility. First and foremost, you should know much more about your products and services —as well as your competitors' products and services — than your prospects. Secondly, you should know your customers' organisation and industry and the unique challenges and issues they face better than any of your competitors. Lastly, "I don't know" is a very appropriate answer when that is, indeed, the case. If you're new to a market, letting your potential customers know that up-front will help lower their expectations and make you feel more comfortable when giving "I don't know" as an answer. When you use this response, however, make sure you offer to find out the answer in a specified timeframe, and then be sure to keep that promise.

4. *Live within your means.* It's simple. Don't force yourself into a position where you "have to make the sale" or you lose something. For one, prospects don't like to feel like you are desperate for business. Secondly, if you want to sell using an honourable approach, it's important to reduce the risk/reward for a given sales situation. If you typically make only three to five sales per year and find yourself in serious debt, don't you think there's a definite likelihood that you might "stretch your value structure" a bit to make sure you win the sale so that your debt can be reduced?
5. *Focus on helping the prospect rather than making the sale.* If all you're thinking about is making the sale, this will be perceived negatively by your prospect through your actions. It doesn't mean you should never think about the sale, it simply means that you need to focus on the prospect's needs first and foremost.
6. *View yourself as an advisor.* This is a different mindset that may be foreign to a lot of sales people. If you adopt the mindset that you're an advisor with the primary goal of identifying and fulfilling your potential customers needs, your attitudes and actions will be perceived very differently by your counterpart(s) than if your view yourself as a sales rep needing to "overcome the obstacles" and "close the sale."
7. *Focus on the long-term.* Admittedly, this is difficult. Most sales people are used to the frequent calls from sales managers reminding them that "we've got to make our monthly or quarterly targets." If you can adopt this attitude, though, you will likely see higher sales, both short-term and long-term. Buyers hate to be "closed." If you take a short-term mentality, there's a high likelihood that buyers will

perceive you as trying to close them — this is trust-breaking and your sales will likely suffer in the short and long-term.

8. *Some business is not worth pursuing.* Most sales managers probably hate this one. It's important, though, to be realistic about each sales opportunity. You're not going to win every sale, so why work under the assumption that you will? Oftentimes, there are many early indicators that will lead you to believe that there's a low probability for making the sale. If that's the case, move on and spend your limited time and energy on opportunities where there's a higher probability for success.
9. *Tell the prospect if your product or service will not meet their needs.* Once you've had a reasonable opportunity to ask the appropriate questions, you must be willing to let the prospect know, as soon as possible, if your product or service will not meet their needs. This will result in a more efficient buy/sell process and save both you and the prospect valuable time that could be better spent elsewhere. The prospect will respect and probably trust you more for selling in this manner, and very well may purchase or recommend someone else to purchase from you in the future.
10. *Ask questions, listen, and take notes.* Entire books have been written on this subject. Prior to every prospect meeting, you should already have a list of at least one dozen questions to ask. The prospect's response to each of these questions should oftentimes be followed by one to three additional questions to drill down to the true issues and needs. Always take notes. This will show the prospect that you're truly listening. Also, send your typed notes to the prospect and ask them to review to ensure that you did indeed "get it right."

11. *Follow the 80/20 Rule.* When meeting with a potential buyer, you should try to talk 20% of the time and allow them to talk 80% of the time — a lot of sales people and sales managers get this one confused.
12. *Be direct.* Answer buyer questions directly. Why do you think there is such a loss in the public's trust with politicians? How often do they provide a direct answer to a question? Rarely. Just because most politicians set a poor example, doesn't mean you should.
13. *No "closing."* One of the worst things you can do as a salesperson is to spend a lot of time and effort building trust with a prospect, only to destroy your "trust factor" towards the end of a complex sales process. No buyer likes to feel they're being manipulated or "closed." Make a recommendation, preferably with several options for the prospect to consider, and ask them to identify the next steps with a timeline. Tell them you'd really appreciate their business and ask what next steps you can take that will be helpful to them.

2

PACKAGING AND PRICING MY PRODUCT

Packaging and pricing represent a very concrete way to communicate with your target market and express the positioning of your business.

2.1. PACKAGING DESIGN

Package design is more than just the look of the physical wrapper or outer container that a product comes in. Packaging can be the way in which services are bundled together for an intermediate buyer or end user. For physical products, the packaging label or wrapper may represent the product's entire business positioning, list of features and benefits, advertising, and promotion, especially for smaller businesses.

Packaging can be simple cardstock tags printed or stamped in black ink (e.g., on machinery, tools, clothing, etc.), or unique, one-of-a-kind containers that are more valuable than their product contents (e.g., imported, hand-blown crystal oil and vinegar cruets). For service businesses, "packaging" represents the way the firm communicates its sources of uniqueness to buyers and end users. Packaging for service companies can be a collection of logo identifications on clothing, uniforms, tools, stationery, forms, hang tags, and other paraphernalia.

Packaging can also be the unique style in which a company provides its services. For example, certain elite hotels are distinguished by their concierge services as much as by their guest rooms and physical amenities. Consulting companies strive to differentiate themselves with their packages of services by bundling areas of expertise together (e.g., tax return preparation and estate planning services).

Transportation companies (e.g., car rental, bus, train, and airline firms) as well as phone and telecommunications companies offer a combination of both products and services. These industries package their products and services together in promotion and advertising. Packaging design essentials apply to both service and physical product companies and must do all of the following:

1. reflect the business positioning
2. communicate graphic identity
3. reflect target buyer values

2.1.1. Positioning

The unique collection of brand or business values that differentiates the business from the competition is known as "positioning." Packaging designs should communicate the business positioning or unique set of values. Colours are also important to product positioning. For example, red is considered to be the most exciting, noticeable colour on the shelf. Red is a key colour component for Coke, Pepsi, Marlboro, and Folger's Coffee, all products that directly, or indirectly, promise stimulation, excitement, energy, and social acceptance. Blues and greens are considered soothing, calming, and serene.

Yellow is for bright moods and celebrations. Orange is the colour of fire. Black connotes power. Gold and silver connote high value. White is neutral or the colour of purity. Many generic grocery products are packaged in simple white with black block printing to indicate the absence of expensive packaging and to separate them from regular, more expensive national brands.

2.1.2. Graphic Identity

Walk through any store and look at packages on the shelves. Decide which ones catch your eye in any given section, and why. Chances are the majority of packages that stand out have what's called *"graphic identity."* Graphic identity is defined as a unique two- or three-dimensional graphic symbol that may be recognised by target buyers as being associated with a particular brand or business. Sometimes this graphic identity takes the simple form of a unique brand logo or name with unusual letter shapes.

For example, Crisco Oil has an unusual graphic identity in the familiar wreath-shaped window on a blue background. Most consumers readily identify this brand from across the room. However, few can recall that the familiar blue can has many different photos of fried chicken, pie, and other foods within the wreath-shape. Small businesses often cannot afford to advertise or promote at the same levels as larger competitors. Therefore, they need to design graphic identity into their logos and packages to ensure reinforcement of uniqueness and positioning. The package may be the only advertising and business positioning communication a small business has.

2.1.3. Packaging to Reflect Buyer's Values

Knowledge of the target buyer's lifestyle as reflected in

the buyer's activities, opinions, interests, and demographics can be manifested in the package names, label design, package copy, and other key communication points. Colours of the package may reflect the natural colours of the outdoors in various seasons:

— yellow, orange, and green for spring and summer.

— brown, gold, and orange for fall.

— white and silver for winter.

Product features communicated on the package may include:

— 100 percent all-natural (ingredients).

— no preservatives or additives.

— biodegradable wrapper.

Product benefits communicated on the package may include:

— safe energy for the whole family!

— environmentally compatible!

— no stomach upset!

If the manufacturer were interested in using a celebrity on the package and in promotions, choices would be restricted to Non-Hollywood types who reflected the target buyer's values.

2.2. PRICING YOUR PRODUCT

Pricing must reflect not only your costs to produce the product or service at the expected volume, but also the value your customers place on what you offer. What's more, price is a way to differentiate your business from others, especially in the consumer market. The ideal price for any product or service is one that is acceptable to both buyer and seller.

From the buyer's standpoint, the right price is a function of product purchase value and other competitive choices in the markets. From the seller's viewpoint, there are many potential pricing objectives. But the basic concern for almost all small businesses is to price products to maximise both sales and profits, while providing enough margin to take care of applicable marketing and overhead expenses. The following steps are recommended for determination of product pricing for any size business:

1. Analyse the size and composition of your target market.
2. Research price elasticity for your product.
3. Evaluate your product's uniqueness.
4. Select your channels of distribution.
5. Consider product life cycles.
6. Analyse your costs and overhead.
7. Estimate sales at different prices.
8. Consider secondary pricing strategies.
9. Select final pricing levels.

2.2.1. Analysing Size and Composition of Market

In setting prices for your product or service, one of the first calculations you must do is to estimate approximately how large your potential sales volume could be, based on a reasonable assessment of your potential market share in the product category, at different price levels. Knowing the size of the existing market is critical to determining if there are enough customers to establish and grow a business. In an established market, in order to sell your product you must cut into your competitors' market shares.

2.2.1.1. *Secondary market research*

Secondary research is something every student has completed at one time or another, usually by doing library research with books and periodicals for a school report. This is usually the cheapest and easiest type of research for small businesses to conduct. However, it may be less reliable than primary research because the information you obtain was not developed with your particular problem or situation in mind. Nevertheless, for some types of information, secondary market research is the only kind available. Secondary research can be divided into two categories:

1. *External Research*: which involves looking at data gathered by industry experts, trade associations, or companies that specialise in gathering and compiling data about various industries.
2. *Internal Research*: which data gathered by your company for purposes other than market research (e.g., sales reports broken down by product line) but which you can use to gauge what the market will do in the future.

2.2.2. Product Price Elasticity

If demand for your product or service changes significantly with slight changes in price, the product category is considered to be *elastic* with respect to price. If no significant volume changes occur, even with significant price changes, the category is *inelastic*. The greater the price elasticity, the closer you should price your products to similar competitive products and vice-versa.

While your product may be unique, consumers will not pay much of a premium for it if there are similar competitive choices at lower prices. To find out more about price elasticity in your industry, study secondary data sources for share and volume results correlated with brand pricing reductions. Talk to trade and association experts to obtain a feel for pricing elasticity.

2.2.3. Evaluation of Product's Uniqueness

The closer your product resembles competitive products, the smaller the price differences that buyers will tolerate. And the closer the product differences between brands, the greater the probability is that the category is price-elastic, and that brand-switching will occur when products go on sale. It is not enough for a product to be unique. The sources of product uniqueness must be both recognisable and valued by buyers. And depending upon the category, very unique products may or may not be readily accepted by buyers.

For example, gourmet food products have many distinct and unique attributes in any given category. Buyers shop for gourmet products because they are often looking for new, unique products — "something out of the ordinary." However, the majority of products sold through mass merchandise stores, grocery stores, chain stores, and vending outlets are easily substituted from among many similar brands. Sources of brand uniqueness are generally very small differences. Usually, buyers aren't looking for new or unique items in these categories.

Product uniqueness does not guarantee a significant price premium over a competitive product, if the product differences aren't recognisable and meaningful to consumers. And depending upon the category, even recognisable and meaningful product differences may not be enough to get buyers to switch to the new product, even at parity pricing, let alone at a premium price over the competition. Field testing on a small market basis is highly recommended for questionable new product differences and unique new products.

2.2.4. Channels of Distribution

Small businesses may have products that would appeal to many different markets or channels of distribution in a single market. However, when you have limited resources, it's often best to select a single distribution channel or a limited number of distribution channels that offer:

1. Greatest ease of entry against the competition.
2. Lowest costs of entry compared to the competition.
3. Least financial risk and commitment to the trade.
4. Sufficient volume potential to reach short-term company goals.
5. Pricing levels to provide acceptable company revenues and profit margins.

2.2.5. Life Cycles of Product

Many product categories have significant evolution and life cycles that may affect pricing decisions. For example, with personal computers and software, the trend is toward shorter and shorter product life cycles. In fact, it now takes as little as six to 12 months before new technology and products are introduced in these multibillion dollar categories. As a result, product pricing cycles have also accelerated to match, with introductory pricing decreasing to significantly lower levels only six to eight months later. These continuously evolving high-tech categories make it difficult for companies to recover development costs, accurately predict sales volume, afford planned marketing support, and price products accurately in relation to a competitor's products.

The most common errors in pricing are:

1. Pricing products or services based only on the cost to produce them.
2. Pricing products based only on competitors' prices.

Several objectives need to be addressed in determining correct product pricing:

1. Cover the cost of producing the goods or services.
2. Cover marketing and overhead expenses.
3. Provide profit objectives.
4. Afford distribution margin discounts.
5. Afford sales commissions.
6. Be competitive.

2.2.5.1. Breakeven analysis

Breakeven analysis is a commonly used method that focuses on the volume of sales at which total revenues will equal total costs. The idea is to set the price of a unit of product or service at a level where it will cover all of its own variable costs (material, labour, marketing etc.) plus its portion of the fixed costs of the company (overhead). At the point where enough units have been sold to cover all fixed and variable costs, breakeven is achieved. After that point, the sales price of a unit sold minus the variable (direct) cost to produce it equals pure profit.

2.2.6. Cost of Consumer Goods

Consumer goods experts suggest the estimated cost of goods should be no more than 15 percent of the suggested retail price because:

— margins of 55 percent to 65 percent are suggested for gross profit to cover:

- — overhead.
- — marketing spending support (e.g., 10 percent to 20 percent of sales).
- — broker commissions (e.g., 5 percent to 10 percent of net sales).
- — your own company profits.
- — a 30 percent margin for distributors who sell to retail stores.
- — a 30 percent to 40 percent margin for retailers on retail prices.

Many other industries, such as restaurants, other retail establishments, and consulting services, operate on the "keystone" pricing principle:

1. The cost of goods is limited to 33 percent, or one-third of retail prices.
2. Labour and overhead is limited to another 33 percent of retail prices.
3. Gross profits are a minimum of 33 percent of retail prices.

2.2.7. Wholesaling and Retailing

Retailers and wholesalers need to consider the issue of markups in their pricing structure, and manufacturers or other product producers need to be aware of the average markup in their industry. A "markup" is the percentage of the selling price (or sometimes the cost) of a product which is added to the cost in order to arrive at a selling price. "Markdown" is a percentage reduction from the selling price.

Be aware that there are two different ways to calculate markup — on cost or on selling price. So when you ask someone "what's your markup on that item?" the answer you want is not just "20 percent," for example, but "20 percent of *cost*" or "20 percent of *selling price*." In retailing, the industry standard is to compute markup as a percentage of selling price. As a product wends its way through a distribution channel, each step along the journey adds a markup before selling the product to the next step.

Markups vary widely among industries. For example, average markups (on selling price in these cases) are 14 percent on tobacco products, 50 percent on greeting cards, 8 percent on baby food and often more than 50 percent on high-end meats. Markups, like all pricing strategies, depend on three influences — *cost*, *competition*, and *demand*.

2.2.8. Estimating Sales at Different Prices

The probability of significant sales volume differences at different prices depends upon the price elasticity of the market and number of similar competitors. First, you'll determine how many similar direct competitors you have and their pricing differences. Perceived value is also important in many categories. Strict price per unit or ounce comparisons may not be meaningful to buyers, if they perceive that one product is of much higher quality than another. Second, determine price elasticity, or "price sensitivity" for the market.

If you have a price-sensitive category and large volume differences occur at various price differences with products on sale, it still may be difficult to accurately measure price versus volume differentials since other factors may also come into play. The length of time various brands have been on the market, their relative market share, brand loyalty factors, advertising and promotion spending levels, sales support, merchandising efforts, distribution penetration levels/market all have an influence on the pricing versus volume equation. In addition, internal company objectives need to be addressed:

1. Cost of goods.
2. Marketing spending.
3. Overhead.
4. Sales commissions.
5. Distributor markups.
6. Shipping costs to distributors.
7. Profit objectives.

Pricing at different levels to generate different volume levels may not address benchmark company objectives. Pricing must cover all costs, spending, and margin objectives.

2.2.9. Other Pricing Objectives and Strategies

In addition to the primary goal of making money, a company can have many different pricing objectives and strategies. Larger companies may utilise product pricing in a predatory or defensive fashion, to attack or defend against a competitor. If you have a premium-quality product, with premium packaging, graphics, and unique features and benefits, perhaps a premium price is necessary to reinforce the premium brand image. Higher margins than normal may be one benefit. High prices confirm perceptions of high value in consumer minds.

A good pricing strategy will also indicate guidelines for action in the case of price increases or decreases. For example, "We will price at or near the share leader's pricing on a per unit basis. We will increase prices to follow a share leader price increase, but only to preserve margin objectives." Strategically, you may want to consider temporarily delaying necessary price increases driven by supplier and ingredient price increases. Take affordable, smaller profit margins if your category segment is price *elastic*. If competitors are increasing prices and your company decides not to, this could be a temporary advantage for your company since sales volume may increase.

2.2.10. Final Price Levels

Final price levels for products should have flexibility for both increases and discounts to customers. Price increases may be inevitable because of component, ingredient, and processing cost increases. The market may or may not absorb price increases without decreasing volume effects. Price decreases due to buyer volume and promotional discounts cannot always be planned for.

Competitors may react to each other with unusual defensive or offensive "deal" programmes that heavily discount pricing to customers for volume purchases. Discount pricing is an often-used tool for market leaders to successfully defend against smaller competitors. Conversely, competitors seeking to gain market share with aggressive offensive low-price discounts may not be successful against a firmly entrenched market leader with loyal customers.

3

SELECTION OF DISTRIBUTION CHANNELS

Selection of distribution channels and sales representation is a method to successful marketing. It's fairly easy to change many of your marketing tactics and strategies on a periodic basis; pricing, packaging, and product mix are among these flexible choices. However, distribution and sales decisions, once made, are much more difficult to change. And distribution affects the selection and utilisation of all other marketing tools.

3.1. TYPES OF DISTRIBUTION CHANNELS

There is a wide variety of possible distribution channels, including:

1. Retail outlets owned by your company or by an independent merchant or chain.
2. Wholesale outlets of your own or those of independent distributors or brokers.
3. Sales force compensated by salary, commission, or both.
4. Direct mail via your own catalogue or flyers.
5. Telemarketing on your own or through a contract firm.

6. Cybermarketing, surfing the newest frontier.
7. TV and cable direct marketing and home shopping channels.

3.2. STEPS FOR SELECTING DISTRIBUTION AND SALES FORCE REPRESENTATION

Distribution choices for a service business follow the same lines as those for a physical product. For example, financial planning services may be offered from printed material, sold at retail by consultants, delivered electronically by computer, or relayed by phone, fax or mail. Steps for selecting distribution and sales force representation include:

1. Identify how competitors' products are sold.
2. Analyse strengths, weaknesses, opportunities, and threats for your business.
3. Examine costs of channels and sales force options.
4. Determine which distribution options match your overall marketing strategy.
5. Prioritise your distribution choices.

Small businesses may face a particular difficulty in identifying their *directly* competitive selling channels, not usually in identifying *where* target buyers buy competitive products. Small companies should make a list of any competitors in their marketing area that could compete *directly* with them for the same list of potential customers. The list of competitors should then be divided into different distribution channels, if applicable. In the architect example, a list of competitors broken down by different local distribution channels includes:

1. Competitors who advertise in local city and county magazines, newspapers, and real-estate flyers, subdivided by home-design only firms and home-design + industrial-design firms.

2. Competitors who work with contractors and developers in the local county.
3. The local university's architectural design department.

Architectural competitors who advertise in local city media may be local, regional or national. In some cases, these competitors solicit home design business from wealthy industrial design clients they are doing work for. Other competitors have contracts to design and modify development-tract homes for local developers. And some competitors work with contractors to design home re-modelling/addition projects. The local university is active in publicising student residential design projects that result in several new home and re-modelling/addition jobs each year.

The development of a list, broken down into competitive distribution channels, can also be assigned estimated dollar sales per year to create market segments. Sales estimates can be gathered by reviewing secondary research data, networking, and attending trade and association events, and by speaking with local government and business organisations (e.g., chamber of commerce and city, state, and federal housing departments, particularly the agency that issues local building permits).

3.3. FACTORS AFFECTING THE DISTRIBUTION

Strength and weakness analysis is an internal company exercise to gauge your ability to compete effectively. Opportunity and threat analysis is an external exercise centred on competitors and the external environment that affect a company's ability to compete effectively. Taken together, they are referred to as SWOT analysis. Each distribution channel alternative and sales force option carries specific costs that can be estimated in most industries and categories. Small businesses need to network with potential or current customers, industry associations, trade suppliers, and competitors to help answer these questions:

1. What are the barriers (difficulties) to entering this product category via each distribution channel?
2. How much do various distribution channels cost to successfully enter? Over what period of time is this money being spent?
3. Should we distribute our business products locally, regionally, nationally? And in what order, or through all channels at the same time?
4. Are some or all of the items we sell subject to varying product life cycles? How do our products compare to competitor product life cycles by channel?
5. What types of competitive spending, promotions, advertising, and field sales response will our business entry encounter by type of distribution channel?

In some categories of small business, other factors should be considered, such as:

1. Ease and affordability of entering the product category.
2. Geographic locations of customers.
3. Existing competitors' market shares.
4. Product life cycle by channel (e.g., vending products may reach saturation in a few months, or have only seasonal distribution).
5. Absolute size of competitors and their financial resources.

3.4. CHOICE OF APPROPRIATE DISTRIBUTION CHANNEL

A small company must work harder at focusing limited resources, especially with distribution and sales force options. In some cases, the only sales force option is for the owner to do it himself or herself, as in a small retail shop, or consulting/service businesses. Some distribution channels and sales force options may be attractive, but off-strategy for the small company. A list of all possible distribution channels and accompanying sales force options should be matched against company marketing objectives.

For example, a company selling gourmet cooking equipment has many options for distribution and sales force representation, including:

1. Company retail stores, with company sales personnel.
2. Specialty food stores, with sales brokers.
3. Department stores, with sales brokers.
4. Hardware stores, with sales brokers.
5. Specialty chains with sales brokers.
6. Direct mail, with company personnel.
7. Distributors, with company sales managers, brokers, distributor sales reps.

The company's products are positioned as the highest-quality cookware, used by celebrity chefs and guaranteed for the life of the end user/buyer. Target end users/buyers are upscale, well-educated, urban consumers who read upscale food magazines, dine out at gourmet restaurants, drink wine, travel, drive expensive cars, and spend heavily on luxury purchases. Ideally, the company wants their products distributed through every upscale channel that caters to this exclusive target group. Because of the positioning of the gourmet cookware, the company believed that hardware stores and direct mail were not consistent with the image and reputation that they were trying to establish with their positioning.

Company retail stores, while desirable, were financially risky and too expensive at the early stage of development. Distributors were also eliminated because of the time and knowledge required of distributor sales personnel, coupled with the belief that distributors could not be encouraged to learn enough or devote enough time to the product line. In addition, the estimated 35 percent to 40 percent discount with shipping expense to distributors was financially unattractive. The company decided the best distribution channels were direct sales to specialty stores and upscale department stores such as Marshall Field's, Bloomingdale's, and Nieman-Marcus. Their sales force consisted of three regional managers with professional cooking experience, who also did demos in stores with the cookware. In addition, the company had the extra margin available to afford this highly trained and motivated sales force since distributors were not utilised.

In some cases, a small business can pursue distribution into several different channels. However, most small businesses must prioritise distribution channel and sales force options over several years of growth and evolving resources for the company. For example, food supplements and vitamins are sold through a multitude of channels, including:

1. Multi-level "network" organisations, with company and independent sales reps.
2. Health food stores, with company reps and sales brokers.
3. Department stores, with company reps and sales brokers.

4. Drug stores, with company reps and sales brokers.
5. Grocery stores, with company reps and sales brokers.
6. Mass merchandise stores, with company reps and sales brokers.
7. Club member warehouse stores, with company reps and sales brokers.
8. Direct mail, with company personnel.
9. Distributors, with company sales managers, brokers, distributor sales reps.
10. Doctors' offices, with company sales managers, brokers, distributor sales reps.

It is not always possible for a company, small or large, to take advantage of all possible channels that match the marketing strategy it wants to achieve. Financial considerations aside, it may be wise to prioritise the orderly development and attack each distribution channel in order of easiest entry and least competitive resistance, for example. Other factors such as geographic proximity, ability and availability of management to control many different channels simultaneously, availability of experienced sales reps, marketing experience by channel, competitive strengths by channel, manufacturing capacities, and product life cycles by channel should be considered.

For small companies, key factors to prioritise your choice of channels include a shorter list:

1. Financial resources and risks.
2. Competitors' strengths and market share.
3. Management experience by channel.
4. Product positioning to target buyers.

4

POSITIONING MY PRODUCT

Positioning is the technique by which marketers try to create an image or identity for a product, brand, or organisation. It is the 'place' a product occupies in a given market as perceived by the target market. Positioning is something that is done in the minds of the target market. A product's position is how potential buyers see the product. Positioning is expressed relative to the position of competitors. Positioning includes identifying the unique market position, or "niche", for your organisation. Positioning is accomplished through market analysis.

Market analysis includes finding out what groups of potential customers (or markets) exist, what groups of customers you prefer to serve (target markets), what their needs are, what products or services you might develop to meet their needs, how the customers might prefer to use the products and services, what your competitors are doing, what pricing you should use and how you should distribute products and services to your target markets. Various methods of market research are used to find out information about markets, target markets and their needs, competitors, etc.

Positioning is a perceptual location. It's where your product or service fits into the marketplace. Effective positioning puts you first in line in the minds of potential customers. As individuals, we continually position ourselves. The responsible older sibling, the class clown, a number cruncher, a super genius are all examples of positioning. These identifiers help us define ourselves and distinguish our abilities as unique and different from other people. Positioning is a powerful tool that allows you to create an image. And image is the outward representation of being who you want to be, doing what you want to do, and having what you want to have.

4.1. PRIMARY ELEMENTS OF POSITIONING

Positioning yourself can lead to personal fulfilment. Being positioned by someone else restricts your choices and limits your opportunities. That's why it's so important for entrepreneurs to transform their passion into a market position. If *you* don't define your product or service, a competitor will do it for you. Your position in the market place evolves from the defining characteristics of your product. The primary elements of positioning are:

1. *Pricing*: Is your product a luxury item, somewhere in the middle, or cheap?
2. *Quality*: Total quality is a much used and abused phrase. But is your product well produced? What controls are in place to assure consistency? Do you back your quality claim with customer-friendly guarantees, warranties, and return policies?
3. *Service*: Do you offer the added value of customer service and support? Is your product customised and personalised?
4. *Distribution*: How do customers obtain your product? The channel or distribution is part of positioning.

5. *Packaging*: Packaging makes a strong statement. Make sure it's delivering the message you intend.

4.2. CHARACTERISTICS OF A GOOD POSITION

A good position is:

1. What makes you unique.
2. This is considered a benefit by your target market.

Both of these conditions are necessary for a good positioning. Positioning is important because you are competing with all the noise out there competing for your potential fans attention. If you can stand out with a unique benefit, you have a chance at getting their attention. It is important to understand your product from the customers point of view relative to the competition.

In order to begin positioning a product, two questions need to be answered:

1. What is our marketing environment?
2. What is our competitive advantage?

The marketing environment is the external environment. Some things to consider:

1. How is the market now satisfying the need your software satisfies?
2. What are the switching costs for potential users for your market?
3. What are the positions of the competition?

4.3. POSITIONING STRATEGIES

The ability to spot a positioning opportunity is a sure test of a person's marketing ability. Successful positioning strategies are usually rooted in a product's sustainable competitive advantage.

The most common basis for constructing a product positioning strategy are:

1. Positioning on specific product features.
2. Positioning on specific benefits, needs, or solutions.
3. Positioning on specific use categories.
4. Positioning on a reason to choose an offering over the competition.
5. Positioning on specific usage occasions.
6. Positioning against another product.
7. Positioning through product class dissociation.
8. Positioning by cultural symbols.

4.4. SEGMENTATION

There are three types of segmentation:

1. *Mass Marketing or Undifferentiated Marketing*: Go after the whole market with one offer and focus on common needs rather than differences
2. *Product-variety Marketing or Differentiated Marketing*: Target several market segments and design separate offers for each
3. *Target Marketing or Concentrated Marketing*: Large share of one or a few sub-markets. Good when company's resources are limited

To identify a niche market, a series of 2 by 2 matrixes can be used to identify an area that is being overlooked by larger competitors. The competitors are mapped on this matrix and you can see where there may be some opportunities.

4.5. POSITIONING DIFFERENCES

The differences that are promoted for a product must be:

1. *Important*: The difference delivers a highly valued benefit to the target buyers.
2. *Distinctive*: Competitors do not offer the difference, or the company can offer it in a more distinctive way.
3. *Superior*: The difference is superior to other ways that the customer might obtain the same benefit.
4. *Communicable*: The difference can be explained and communicated to the target buyers.
5. *Preemptive*: Competitors cannot easily copy the difference.
6. *Affordable*: Buyers can afford to pay the difference.
7. *Profitable*: Company can introduce the difference profitably.

Positioning is a new approach to communication, advertising and marketing. It is an organised system for finding a window in the mind of your prospect in order to position effectively over there a product - a merchandise, a service, a company, or a person - against its main competitors. This system is based on the concept that communication can only take place at the right time and under the right circumstances. The mind accepts only that new information which matches its current state. It filters out everything else.

In other words, positioning is a process by which a psychological "anchor" has been placed into the minds of prospects so that they come to choose one specific person or company over another. Positioning is what you do to the mind of the prospect - you look for the solution of your problem inside the prospect's mind. Anyone can use positioning strategy to get ahead in the game of life. You must realise that your product or service cannot be all things to all people. Very few items on the market today have universal appeal.

Even when dealing in basic commodities like table salt or aspirin, marketing people have gone to all sorts of extremes to create brand awareness and product differentiation. If your product or service is properly positioned, prospective purchasers or users should immediately recognise its unique benefits or advantages and be better able to assess it in comparison to your competition's offering. Positioning is how you give your product or service brand identification. Positioning involves analysing each market segment as defined by your research activities and developing a distinct position for each segment. Ask yourself how you want to appear to that segment, or what you must do for that segment to ensure that it buys your product or service. This will dictate different media and advertising appeals for each segment.

For example, you may sell the same product in a range of packages or sizes, or make cosmetic changes in the product, producing private labels or selecting separate distribution channels to reach the various segments. Beer, for example, is sold on tap and in seven-ounce bottles, twelve-ounce cans and bottles, six-packs, twelve-packs, cases, and quart bottles and kegs of several sizes. The beer is the same but each package size may appeal to a separate market segment and have to be sold with a totally different appeal and through different retail outlets.

Remember that your marketing position can, and should, change to meet the current conditions of the market for your product. The ability of your company to adjust will be enhanced greatly by an up-to-date knowledge of the marketplace gained through continual monitoring. By having good data about your customers, the segments they fit into and the buying motives of those segments, you can select the position that makes the most sense.

4.6. CATEGORIES OF MARKETING POSITIONS

While there are many possible marketing positions, most would fit into one of the following categories:

1. *Positioning on specific product features*: A very common approach, especially for industrial products. If your product or service has some unique features that have obvious value this may be the way to go.
2. *Positioning on benefits*: Strongly related to positioning on product features. Generally, this is more effective because you can communicate to your customers about what your product or service can do for them. The features may be nice, but unless customers can be made to understand why the product will benefit them, you may not get the sale.
3. *Positioning for a specific use*: Related to benefit positioning. Consider Campbell's positioning of soups for cooking. An interesting extension is mood positioning: "Have a Coke and a smile." This works best when you can teach your customers how to use your product or when you use a promotional medium that allows a demonstration.
4. *Positioning for user category*: A few examples: "You've Come a Long Way Baby," "The Pepsi Generation" and "Breakfast of Champions." Be sure you show your product being used by models with whom your customers can identify.
5. *Positioning against another product or a competing business*: A strategy that ranges from implicit to explicit comparison. Implicit comparisons can be quite pointed; for example, Avis never mentions Hertz, but the message is clear. Explicit comparisons can take two major forms. The first

form makes a comparison with a direct competitor and is aimed at attracting customers from the compared brand, which is usually the category leader. The second type does not attempt to attract the customers of the compared product, but rather uses the comparison as a reference point.

6. *Product class dis-association*: A less common type of positioning. It is particularly effective when used to introduce a new product that differs from traditional products. Lead-free gasoline and tubeless tires were new product classes positioned against older products. Space-age technology may help you here. People have become accustomed to change and new products and are more willing to experiment than was true ten years ago. Even so, some people are more adventure some and trusting than others and more apt to try a revolutionary product. The trick is to find out who are the potential brand switchers or experimenters and find out what it would take to get them to try your product or service. The obvious disadvantage of dealing with those who try new products is that they may move on to another brand just as easily. Brand loyalty is great as long as it is to your brand.
7. *Hybrid bases*: Incorporates elements from several types of positioning. Given the variety of possible bases for positioning, small business owners should consider the possibility of a hybrid approach. This is particularly true in smaller towns where there aren't enough customers in any segment to justify the expense of separate marketing approaches.

The rapid growth of communication methods has given us a new disease: Information Overload Syndrome. In today's over-communicated society, to be successful, you must touch base with reality. And the only reality that counts is what's already in the prospect's mind. In the communication jungle out there, there are just too many products, too many companies, and too much marketing noise. The mind, as a defence against the huge volume of today's communications, screens and rejects much of the information it offered.

The only hope to score big is to be selective, to concentrate on narrow targets, to practice segmentation. In a word, "positioning". The basic approach of positioning is not to create something new and different, but to manipulate what's already up in your prospect's mind, to retie the connection that already exist. The advertising people spend their time and research money looking for positions, or holes, in the marketplace.

4.7. PRODUCT POSITIONING PROCESS

Generally, the product positioning process involves:

1. Identifying competing products.
2. Identifying the attributes (also called dimensions) that define the product 'space'.
3. Collecting information from a sample of customers about their perceptions of each product on the relevant attributes.
4. Determine each products' share of mind.
5. Determine each products' current location in the product space.
6. Determine the target market's preferred combination of attributes.
7. examine the fit between:
   a. the positions of competing products.
   b. the position of your product.
   c. the position of the ideal vector.
   d. select optimum position.

The process is similar for positioning your company's services. Services, however, don't have the physical attributes of products - that is, we can't feel them or touch them or show nice product pictures. So you need to ask first your customers and then yourself, what value do clients get from my services? How are they better off from doing business with me? Also ask: is there a characteristic that makes my services different?

Write out the value customers derive and the attributes your services offer to create the first draft of your positioning. Test it on people who don't really know what you do or what you sell, watch their facial expressions and listen for their response. When they want to know more because you've piqued their interest and started a conversation, you'll know you're on the right track.

4.8. POSITIONING CONCEPTS

More generally, there are three types of positioning concepts:

1. Functional positions.
   a. Solve problems,
   b. Provide benefits to customers.
2. Symbolic positions.
   a. Self-image enhancement,
   b. Ego identification,
   c. Belongingness and social meaningfulness,
   d. Affective fulfilment.
3. Experiential positions.
   a. Provide sensory stimulation,
   b. Provide cognitive stimulation.

4.9. MEASURING THE POSITIONING

Positioning is facilitated by a graphical technique called perceptual mapping, various survey techniques, and statistical techniques like multi dimensional scaling, factor analysis, conjoint analysis, and logit analysis.

There are many ways for a business to be unique, from small pricing, packaging, and service differences to significant feature and benefit contrasts with the competition. In all cases, your business's uniqueness has to be examined in relation to other products and services that your target buyer is currently using (i.e., things that your business hopes to replace with its own offerings). Differences really don't matter unless they are important enough to the customer to influence his or her purchasing decision.

In some cases, there may actually be little or no difference between your product or service and that of your competitors. Or, the differences may be very difficult to communicate (think of the difference between Coke and Pepsi.) In that case, it's up to you to create some differences. For example, granulated white sugar is essentially indistinguishable from one brand to another. Physical product features are the same for each brand. Product benefits and usage are identical. However, even plain white sugar can be differentiated with pricing, packaging, and quality image supported by advertising.

Consumers consistently rank price as one of the most important features of branded granulated sugars in making a purchase decision. Another important feature is the brand image of quality, which reinforces this image with a higher price versus generic brands.

You've already begun the process of thinking about your positioning if you've constructed a unique selling proposition (USP) for your product or business.

Differentiation is the collection of differences in features and benefits versus competitive products. *The key is to determine how important these collective differences are to the buyer.* Communication of important differences is the basis for a successful positioning strategy. Positioning is adding brand value to this collection of differences in the mind of the buyer. In other words, you must solve the problem of how to communicate a *meaningful difference* about your business idea to the people who are most interested in buying it.

Meaningful differences in your product or service, compared to that of your competitors, should be created and communicated to your target buyer via packaging, pricing, features and benefits, product design, colours, advertising and promotion mediums, public relations events, and even spokespersons. Everything should work together to promote a consistent image for your product or service. Correct positioning can be thought of as solving the marketing mix problems of the "Four Ps of Marketing":

1. Product.
2. Price.
3. Promotion or advertising.
4. Place (distribution).

As well as the "Four Cs":

1. Company definition.
2. Competitors' identification.
3. Consumer target definition.
4. Channels.

4.10. STRENGTHENING PRODUCT POSITIONING

Many small companies believe there is little they can do to really position their products and services because they spend little or no money to promote their products to their target buyers. However, almost all products and services come "packaged" in one form or another. Even service businesses have uniforms, logos, slogans, types of vehicles, specialised greetings, service procedures, follow-up procedures, and a host of unique ways to differentiate themselves from their competitors. Packaging is an important way for you to get your positioning message across.

Positioning is ordinarily a very important factor in creating effective advertising and promotion. In fact, the less money spent on advertising and promotion, the more important correct and consistent positioning becomes for a small company's products. Small companies, like large ones, must:

1. Work at consciously identifying brand features and benefits that are unique to differentiate the company and its products from the competition.
2. Communicate and test which differences are most important to buyers and consumers in deciding to purchase your products rather than those of competitors.
3. Work at communicating the most unique and important differences to buyers and consumers to create "branded value" and a "brand personality."

A new competitor could enter the market with the same target buyer and decide to differentiate their new chair by adding a new extra electronic massage feature, provide similar fabrics, a foam-lined crate, a slightly lower price and celebrity spokespersons who promote value along with quality.

Qualitative research such as interviews with a small number of people, or more reliable (but expensive) quantitative research, can be done to determine how buyers and end-users understand and value your business differences with competitors. This research can help generate a unique selling proposition for the business and help create effective advertising and promotion.

A company must be careful not to "overposition," which can be defined as making promises about features and benefits that the product or business does not always deliver. Overpositioning can also mean making promises about product features and benefits that are not apparent to users/buyers. You must also avoid "underpositioning," which can be defined as failing to describe all the features and benefits that the product or business delivers or has, or failing to describe *distinctive* product features and benefits that are apparent to users/buyers.

Also, it's important to avoid confusing people with product or service features and benefits. Features are the descriptors of a product (e.g., colours, smells, shapes, packaging, prices), while benefits are what the product does for its buyers (e.g., satisfaction, more confidence, more beauty, faster task completion). It's often better to single out a few key features, rather than overwhelming the customer with lengthy lists of details.

5

UNDERSTANDING MY CUSTOMER

Understanding one's customers is so important that large corporations spend hundreds of millions annually on market research. Although such formal research is important, a small firm can usually avoid this expense. Typically, the owner or manager of a small concern knows the customers personally. From this foundation, understanding of your customers can be built by a systematic effort. A comprehensive system for understanding is what Rudyard Kipling called his six honest serving men. "Their names are: What and Why and When and How and Where and Who."

5.1. UNDERSTANDING WHAT CUSTOMERS ARE BUYING

A seller characterises what customers are buying as goods and services—toothpaste, drills, video games. But understanding of buyers starts with the realisation that they purchase benefits as well as products. Consumers don't select toothpaste. Instead some will pay for a decay preventive. Some seek pleasant taste. Others want bright teeth. Or perhaps any formula at a bargain price will do. Similarly, industrial purchasing agents are not really interested in drills. They want holes. They insist on quality appropriate for their purposes, reliable delivery when needed, safe operation, and reasonable prices.

Video games are fun. They are bought for home entertainment, family togetherness, development of personal dexterity, introduction to computers, among other satisfactions. Commercial customers include arcades, pizza parlours, and assorted enterprises. They benefit from a potential source of income, a means of attracting buyers to their premises, or perhaps a competitive move. Similarly, cars are visible evidence of a person's wealth, reflection of life style, a private cabin for romance. Or they represent receipts from leases, means to pursue an occupation... Some people even buy cars for transportation.

You must find out, from their point of view, what customers are buying. The common names of products mean as little to them as the chemical names on the label of a proprietary drug. (A sick person's real need is safe and speedy relief.) Understanding your customers enables you to profit by providing what buyers seeks - satisfaction. Products change, but basic benefits like personal hygiene, attractiveness, safety, entertainment, and privacy endure.

So do commercial purposes such as quests for competitive superiority or profitability. Successful manufacturers and service establishments produce benefits for which customers are willing to pay. Successful wholesalers and retailers select offerings of such demanded benefits that they can resell at a profit. Successful business-people, in other words, understand the reason for their customers' buying decisions.

5.2. UNDERSTANDING; WHY CUSTOMERS ARE BUYING?

The reason that customers buy is logical from their point of view. Understanding customers derives from this fundamental premise. Don't argue with taste. Everybody is unique. Each person has individual pressures and criteria. Moreover, perceptions differ. The astute business-person deduces and accepts the buying logic of customers and serves them accordingly.

Some buyers hide their true motivations. In many cases the reasons are obscure to the buyers themselves. Most purchase decisions are multi-causal. Often, conflicts abound. A car buyer may want the roominess of a large vehicle and the fuel economy of a subcompact. The resolution of such mutually exclusive desires is usually indeterminate. Sometimes the reasons why customers buy are trivial.

If customers feel indifferent toward a product or store, the selection is apt to be happenstance. Perhaps several rival offerings meet all the conditions that a purchaser deems important. Consequently, minor factors govern. This explains the rationale of the consumer who chose a $ 22,000 car because its upholstery was most attractive. The point: Pay attention to details. They may be crucial to customers. Often the best clues are the customers' actions. Shrewd business-people respect what people say, but pay special attention to what people do.

More important than why customers buy is why former customers have taken their patronage elsewhere and why qualified buyers are not buying. What is now keeping them from buying? Can this obstacle be surmounted? Business-people monitor competitive offerings and buyers' reactions to infer clues. Informal conversations may also reveal some reasons. Special offers may overcome resistance and boost profits. All the time the manager must be careful to retain the company's regular customers.

For instance, a specialty dress shop may try to widen its patronage through a new line at bargain prices. This move could disturb the store's usual patrons. They may take their trade to another store that caters exclusively to their social class. Many of the dresses were bought for special occasions when projection of a genteel image was important to the customer. Understanding of customers includes awareness of the time of the purchase and use of the merchandise.

5.3. UNDERSTANDING WHEN CUSTOMERS ARE BUYING

A seller must be ready when the buyer is, lest an opportunity be irretrievably lost. Customers buy when they want an offering and have the time and money to purchase it. Buying patterns can often be discerned from an analysis of customers and their purchases. For example, wants for many consumer goods and services are tied to customers' rites of passage. The following purchase occasions in the adult life cycle are typical:

1. Marriage, separation, divorce.
2. Acquisition of a home.
3. Change in employment or career.
4. Graduate study.
5. Health care, injury, illness.
6. Pregnancy, nurture of children.
7. Children enter school; graduate.
8. Children leave home.
9. Move to another area.
10. Vacations; major social activities.
11. Permanent retirement from work.
12. Death of a family member.

Shrewd retailers keep track of such key buying events and gain a head start on making sales. Logs of birthdays and anniversaries are a case in point. Additional purchase occasions are impersonal. Seasonal factors include recurring holidays and weather changes. Among other favourable influences on purchases are start of the school year, semi-annual white sales, introduction of new models and clearance of old ones, special price concessions, and improvement in economic conditions or buyer's confidence.

Some of the latter factors also apply to manufacturers. Small plants work closely with their buyers' inventory managers and replenish stock at their reorder point. A current vogue is just-in-time delivery. Interactive computers make replenishment notices routine. Many consumers have time for shopping only during off-hours in the evenings, and on weekends. The trend from a single breadwinner per family toward having all adults of a household engage in commercial employment has intensified this time peculiarity.

Astute retailers adjust their hours, staffing, and availability of merchandise to customers' shopping convenience. Bartenders know that business booms on payday. Manufacturers profit from timing their offers to their customers' budgetary cycles. Thus, knowing when products are bought and used is a valuable facet of understanding customers. Although a transaction may be concluded in a moment, most purchases actually entail a drawn-out process.

5.4. UNDERSTANDING; HOW CUSTOMERS AREBUYING?

Knowledge of how customers buy pays off in several ways.

1. Sellers can design their offerings to meet the exact needs of their buyers.
2. Sellers can influence decision makers at crucial steps of the buying process.
3. Sellers can lay the groundwork for repeat business.

Buying methods are best visualised as processes. Household purchases usually start when a consumer has a desire or a problem that an acquisition might satisfy or solve. Industrial purchases usually start when a user or a routine sets off a signal (requisition) for approval of a procurement.

People are diverse. Every consumer, every firm pursues a buying process of its own. Buying processes also depend on the significance of the product to the buyer and on other circumstances. Although buying processes are not uniform some steps are common to most of them. The seller needs to know only these critical steps when he or she can affect the outcome of the buying decision. Shrewd sellers delve into the behavioural milestones of purchasers. But for each very important customer the buying process should be diagrammed individually, showing names of influencers at each decision stage, elapsed time between stages, and any other pertinent information.

Perhaps a change in life style or a demonstration at a friend's house has caused this consumer to recognise the need for a personal computer. But lack of knowledge and the fear of a wrong decision may counteract this desire. The process continues, however, if advertisements and expected benefits persuade the consumer to act. Despite budgetary constraints and uncertainty about future needs, the consumer proceeds to compare stores and brands. At this search and evaluation stage advice from present satisfied customers is especially influential.

Make sure your customers are satisfied and favourably recommend your merchandise or service. To the contrary, poor shopping facilities or irritating personnel can sway the potential customer against making the purchase from you. Sooner or later, further search does not seem worthwhile. If the positives still outweigh the negatives, the consumer picks a store and brand. The transaction itself is consummated quickly, assuming the wanted item is available. The satisfied customer makes recommendations to others and gives you his or her repeated, regular business.

Business-people can create sales by predisposing potential buyers to their product or store. Manufacturers can offer exclusive benefits in their goods, such as friendly relations, efficient operations, and easy manuals. Enticing advertisements help persuade prospects to visit a retail outlet and ask about a particular brand. Creative salespeople overcome the customer's objections and doubts and close the sale. Post-transaction service keeps the customer satisfied. Referrals usually follow.

Specific details are needed to track acquisition of something complex, say a computer. On the other hand, less detail is needed if the purchase is laundry detergent or some other staple with which the customer is less involved. In the latter case, depletion of the home inventory triggers a routine, leading directly to choice: the usually purchased brand. If the usual brand is out-of-stock or another brand is on sale a substitute may be bought quickly. Brand comparisons follow or may be omitted.

Some products are bought when an emergency need for them arises. A physical examination and the filling of a prescription are urgent when sickness strikes. Arrangements for funerals follow immediately after the death of a family member. Umbrellas are in demand when it rains. An unexpected snow storm generates extra calls for tire chains, towing services, and car batteries. Often, convenient availability determines when these goods and services are purchased. And even if customers do have ample time to select merchandise, sellers who stand ready to supply wanted or expected brands are apt to gain preference and profit when shoppers decide where to buy.

People want options. Although convenient availability is the main buying criterion for many routine household products, savvy merchants stock a selection conforming to the diverse preferences of their patrons. Some people demand manufacturers' advertised brands. Resellers' brands are favoured by others. On some classes of goods, generic brands have become popular in recent years. Moreover, many consumers seek occasional variety. Clearly the decision of which products to stock is important. It is more important yet on shopping goods because buyers compare them before purchase. And it is most important on specialty goods, those preselected by brand name. If a store does not stock these uniquely wanted brands, a prospect will leave without buying. Whoever offers them on acceptable terms gains the sale.

5.5. UNDERSTANDING; FROM WHERE CUSTOMERS ARE BUYING

From a multitude of studies emerge different criteria for deciding where to shop. Most research on the subject agrees that store location is a major consideration, Stores usually draw most of their patronage from their surrounding neighbourhood. Savvy store managers make a special effort to understand the shopping-related motivations and preferences of local residents. New managers of fast-food units, for example, canvass nearby dwellings and introduce themselves to the households.

Some supermarkets maintain consumer advisory boards to elicit suggestions and reactions. Other means of communication with customers include informal conversations at the store and suggestion boxes with interviews and awards. Incidentally, complaints are an excellent guide for making store policies more amenable to customers. Personnel should be instructed to thank patrons for their comments. Prompt consideration, followed by a personal letter from the store manager, is highly desirable.

Location is extremely important to "captive" buyers. Exclusively franchised utilities, shops in isolated hotels and cafeterias or automatic vending machines in factories are examples. At the opposite extreme, shoppers escape spatial restrictions by buying from mail-order firms or telephone solicitors. Other patronage influences vary. They depend on the type of product, type of store, and the characteristics of the consumer. The offered assortment's perceived quality, depth, and breadth certainly are very important, along with price. This does not imply that all goods have to be top quality or all prices the lowest. Perceptions are decisive.

If quality seems high, some customers infer that prices are high too regardless of the facts. The important point is to understand customers and to provide what causes them to buy. For example, assurance of repair service weighs heavily with the worrier type of customer. A convenience-minded buyer is concerned with parking space or delivery service. Of course, shoppers must be told that wanted goods and services are available. Advertising helps disseminate this information. So does a store's reputation for consistent policies of satisfying its customers.

Occasional promotions inject some excitement into the tedium of shopping. Some clients like to socialise, which can absorb much of an employee's time and may even annoy other buyers. Nevertheless, personnel should be friendly and helpful. Also influential, for some customers, is the apparent socio-economic level of other shoppers. Personal affinity for other customers or for salespeople is a decisive factor in the success of party-selling, e.g., household goods and in-home selling (cosmetics). The choice of where to buy items requiring major outlays (securities, and insurance) often revolves around from whom to buy.

In selecting a retail store, many customers consider physical features. Layouts can invite or repel patronage. Motorists who are in a hurry, for instance, are apt to use a gasoline station at which business can be transacted quickly. Altogether, buyers perceive a mix of tangible and intangible factors that comprise a store's atmosphere. Accordingly, they either do or don't feel comfortable about shopping there.

5.6. UNDERSTANDING; WHO ARE BUYING—IDENTIFICATION OF CUSTOMERS?

Identification of customers and prospects makes effective targeting possible. Small business owners pride themselves on knowing their customers personally. In the industrial field, understanding of each major customer and buying influence is essential. When dealing with a large number of customers, however, individual familiarity is not feasible. Hence mass merchandisers and others in this situation group their customers, whose reactions to offerings are similar, into segments. Then they design a separate appropriate marketing programme for each segment. Strategies vary, a small firm might prosper by concentrating its resources on one segment. Because customers are volatile, the specialising firm is vulnerable to sudden change in its target segment's patronage.

Hence some companies address several segments simultaneously. Although expensive, a strategy of employing different tactics for different segments can be quite profitable. Other firms scatter offers to just anybody. They hope that segments will select themselves. One basis for segmentation is geographic. Retail customers are apt to live or work in the store's vicinity.

Industrial buyers tend to concentrate regionally. So do users of services. Intensive cultivation of local potential customers can be efficient and lucrative. Personal knowledge of local buyers and a shared community spirit help cement relations with these customers.

Segmentation is an art. All "honest serving men" - what, why, when, how, where, as well as who - can be the key to segmentation. Whatever the basis, each identified segment should have sufficient purchasing power to make a special effort commercially worthwhile. Accessibility is vital. How can the segment be reached? Are advertisements, telephone solicitations, or personal visits efficient? How about trade shows or personal contacts? The ideal segment is stable in purchase needs and loyalty, helping you fend off competition.

Besides segmentation, understanding of customers also requires insight into their buying roles. The buyer for a one-person household or one-person business is the initiator of the order, the decider, and the user. Even in this case, however, some outsiders are influential. In larger households or businesses, these buying roles are usually played by separate individuals. It helps you to know who activates (requisitions) purchases, who exerts influence, who decides what and where to buy, who uses the product and what their criteria are. Then you tailor and target your offerings to satisfy each major participant in the buying process.

A small firm that understands its customers can buy or produce exactly what they want-and nothing else. The firm's sales effort is efficient because it builds on why its customers want to buy not on why others buy, or why the vendor wants to sell. Merchandise can be ready when customers need it. Thus a knowledgeable seller avoids unnecessary inventory costs or penalties for late delivery. Understanding how customers buy lets a seller employ promotional media, appeals, and timing for maximum effectiveness. Transportation costs are lowered by shipping merchandise to where it is needed. Knowledge of who comprises suitable segments and the separate buying roles can reduce the waste of soliciting unqualified or uninterested people.

The best source for you to learn about customers is your personal interaction with them. At work, social and civic activities, and chance encounters, people talk and reveal their attitudes and motivation. Listen to your customers. You can also keep abreast of purchasing patterns by observing competitors' practices and by asking sales personnel who is buying what, where. Articles in business and trade newspapers and magazines give information on products, trends, marketing, finance, the economy. Trade directories, Yellow Pages, and brokers' direct-mail lists identify who buyers are, and most industries have associations and specialised marketing research that provide insights for understanding customers.

5.7. UNDERSTANDING; CUSTOMER NEEDS

Understanding customer needs will help you define new market opportunities and drive innovation and revenue growth in every aspect of your organisation. In the new rapidly changing economy, however, customer predictability is dead. "Whatever a customer wants today may not be what he or she wants tomorrow. Or he or she may want more of it. If you're offering low prices, customers want those prices slashed further. If you're offering state-of-the art products, they want them newer still. In meeting ever-increasing customer demands for lower, faster, better, and newer, companies are driving themselves and their competitors to the brink." You can't predict the future, but by establishing effective change management practices you can be ready for whatever it brings.

If you want to develop a new product or service, exploratory market and customer research should be an essential and continuous component of the process. It provides the foundation and platform for effective idea generation and creativity management. "It describes customer or consumer needs, wants, gripes, complaints, and problems that each have about the performance of a certain activity, function, process, life event, or product. This research, prior to idea generation, provides the basis for setting up a problem-solving mindset towards idea generation." To explore customer needs and wants, examine external market and competitive trends, ascertain potential needs and wants of each customer segment and character type, identify problems that customer cite, observe people to discover their unrealised needs.

Historically, holiday shopping has been about finding the best deal. But using technology to gain knowledge of customer needs can encourage them to buy on features rather than on sale. Retail technology has often been touted as a way to cut costs by eliminating overstocking and forced sales. It does all that, and does it well. Beyond using customer information to ensure that your displays are stocked with the right products, priced at whatever the market will bear, technology can also help you ensure that customers have the most hassle-free shopping experience possible.

That time of year that retailers both dread and anticipate is quickly approaching. Yes, the holiday shopping season is once again almost upon us. Obviously increased business is always welcome, but the pressures attendant on this make-or-break time of year can crush any flicker of festive spirit. The economy may have stabilised, but consumers aren't yet in the mood to cast caution to the wind and spend as if there's no tomorrow. Traditionally, the way to woo cautious shoppers has been to offer a large stock of aggressively priced products.

Retail technology has often been touted as a way to cut costs by eliminating overstocking and forced sales. It does all that, and does it well. But it also offers a sometimes-overlooked benefit customer service. Beyond using customer information to ensure that your displays are stocked with the right products, priced at whatever the market will bear, technology can also help you ensure that customers have the most hassle-free shopping experience possible.

6

DIRECT SELLING OF MY PRODUCT

Direct selling is a dynamic, vibrant, rapidly expanding channel of distribution for the marketing of products and services directly to consumers. Direct selling can best be described as the marketing of products and services directly to consumers in a face to face manner, generally in their homes or the homes of others, at their workplace and other places away from permanent retail locations. Direct sales typically occur through explanation or personal demonstration by an independent direct salesperson. These salespersons are commonly referred to as direct sellers.

6.1. STRENGTH OF DIRECT SELLING

The strength of direct selling lies in its tradition of independence, service to consumers, and commitment to entrepreneurial growth in the free market system. Direct selling provides accessible business opportunities to people looking for alternative sources of income, and whose entry is generally not restricted by gender, age, education, or previous experience. It should be noted that around the world a substantial majority of direct sellers are women, and most work in their direct selling businesses on a part-time basis.

A very small percentage of direct sellers are employees of the companies whose products they sell. Independent direct sellers are those individuals engaged on their own behalf, or on behalf of a direct selling company, selling products and services through personal sales contacts, and are commonly referred to in some jurisdictions as independent contractors. Essentially, this means that these independent salespersons are not employed by the company whose products they distribute, but are independent business persons operating their own businesses. These independent direct sellers have an opportunity to earn profits from their business, and also accept the responsibility for the risks associated with operating a business.

The products sold by direct sellers are as diverse as the people themselves and include: cosmetics and skin care products; laundry and personal care items; vacuum cleaners and home appliances; household specialties; household cleaning products; food and nutrition products; toys, books and educational products; and clothing, jewelry and fashion accessories; just to mention a few. Generally, these products are sold in the context of group presentations (Party Plan), or on a person to person basis (one-to-one).

In a Party Plan approach, the direct salesperson demonstrates products to a group of guests, invited by a host in whose home or other location the direct selling demonstration takes place. By contrast, other direct sellers will often explain and demonstrate the products they offer to consumers in the comfort of the consumers' homes, at a time which is convenient for them. Direct selling provides important benefits to individuals who desire an opportunity to earn an income and build a business of their own; to consumers who enjoy an alternative to shopping centers, department stores or the like; and to the consumer products market. It offers an alternative to traditional employment for those who desire a flexible income earning opportunity to supplement their household income, or whose responsibilities or circumstances do not allow for regular part-time or full time employment.

In many cases, direct selling opportunities develop into a fulfilling career for those who achieve success and choose to pursue their independent direct selling business on a full time basis. The cost for an individual to start an independent direct selling business is typically very low. Usually, a modestly priced sales kit is all that is required for one to get started, and there is little or no required inventory or other cash commitments to begin. This stands in sharp contrast to franchise and other business investment opportunities which may require substantial expenditures and expose the investor to a significant risk of loss. Consumers benefit from direct selling because of the convenience and service it provides, including personal demonstration and explanation of products, home delivery, and generous satisfaction guarantees.

Moreover, direct selling provides a channel of distribution for companies with innovative or distinctive products not readily available in traditional retail stores, or who cannot afford to compete with the enormous advertising and promotion costs associated with gaining space on retail shelves. Direct selling enhances the retail distribution infrastructure of the economy, and serves consumers with a convenient source of quality products.

An important component of the direct selling industry is multilevel marketing. It is also referred to as network marketing, structure marketing or multilevel direct selling, and has proven over many years to be a highly successful and effective method of compensating direct sellers for the marketing and distribution of products and services directly to consumers.

Direct selling should not be confused with terms such as direct marketing or distance selling which may be described as an interactive system of marketing that uses one or more advertising media to effect a measurable response and/or transaction at any location, with this activity stored on a database. Some commonly known types of direct marketing and distance selling techniques are telemarketing, direct mail, and direct response. Although direct selling organizations occasionally use some direct marketing or distance selling techniques and technology to enhance their businesses, the primary difference between the two methods of marketing is the face to face, or personal presentation that is always an aspect of the direct selling relationship.

You can sell anything direct, from intangible items such as insurance to high-ticket items such as airplanes. Direct selling is simply salesmanship in print. It allows you to build a direct relationship with prospects over time, irrespective of geography or opening hours. It also allows people to buy from the comfort of their home or office with minimal effort. Direct selling is an increasingly popular sales technique because it cuts out the middleman. Indeed, many companies highlight this in their marketing.

6.2. PLANNING A DIRECT MAILING CAMPAIGN

Direct selling can be expensive. To make it work, you need to be able to gain insight into your prospects, isolating them from the rest of the world, seeing and treating them as individuals with individual needs, drivers and motivators. The degree to which you can do this is measured by how convincing and appealing prospects find your offers. You can also find what works best for you. One great advantage of direct selling is that you can test and then modify your next direct marketing campaign according to the results. You can:

1. Measure the response to particular messages at particular times.
2. Measure such things as whether people prefer opening yellow envelopes to blue ones.
3. Find the optimum price for the volumes of a product you want to sell.

Direct selling is about finding prospects and turning them into customers and turning customers into repeat buyers and, better still, advocates. The key is to build trust and to do this you need to know your prospects intimately. If you are using direct mail, use the right mailing lists. If you are buying space or airtime, use the right media at the right time. If you are using a website, use the right keywords. There are a number of tips you should bear in mind when planning a direct mailing campaign:

1. Remember the acronym AIDA - attract Attention, arouse Interest, create Desire and call for Action.
2. Make people clip that coupon or dial that number now.
3. Focus on benefits. Describe the features of your product or service in relation to benefits. For example: "This car has a five speed gear box (feature) for greater fuel economy (benefit).
4. Prove your benefits. Cite test results, quote experts, use testimonials - prospects are more likely to trust disinterested parties and satisfied buyers than the seller.
5. Use money-back guarantees to soothe prospects' fears that they may be making a mistake. Such guarantees encourage impulse buys.
6. People buy on impulse and rationalise their choices afterwards so identify the key emotions and sales triggers you are appealing to.

7. Be easily contactable. The less hassle it is for consumers to buy, the more likely they are to do so.
8. Make ordering easy and a pleasure. Use polite, friendly staff who answer calls promptly and deal with customers efficiently.
9. Set standards for customer service and fulfilment and communicate this to everyone involved.
10. Plan how you will handle returns and complaints and set up strict procedures. If you can shine here people will learn to trust you.
11. Keep customer information on a database and use the information to cross-sell other products and services.
12. Test every element of the mailing - timing, content, special offers and discounts etc - but only test one at a time.
13. Encourage customer loyalty by offering bonuses to loyal customers. These can include membership of clubs, discounts and free gifts.

It is possible to sell direct and use a middleman. Magazines are good examples of this, where publishers sell via news-stands and sell subscriptions direct. Subscribers pay up front but get the convenience of having the magazine delivered to their door and sometimes other benefits.

On the other hand, not everyone likes to buy at a distance. Indeed, many people like to touch before they buy and, in the case of subscriptions, may not want to pay a year in advance. Direct selling is a powerful medium and has made many people rich. However, many customers still prefer to buy face to face. To be successful at direct selling, plan, test and measure everything.

6.3. DEADLY MISTAKES OF DIRECT MAIL

Now put yourself in the shoes of your direct mail recipients. Avoid direct mail deadly mistakes or your materials will end up in the trash too. Before you even begin to put your direct mail campaign together, you've got to know who your target market is. Are they women? Parents? Young? Old? Understand what motivates them. What are their likes and dislikes? Write as if you're talking to them. And even use terms these types of people would use.

But all the fancy graphics and the most beautifully created sentences in the world won't do you a bit of good if you don't carefully select the people on your mailing list. If you're selling adult diapers, you want to target senior citizens...not 23-year-olds. Tighten your mailing list as much as possible to be sure it's tailored to your needs. It's tough to make people believe they need your product and even harder to convince them they need it now. But if you've researched your list, you have a higher chance of hitting potential customers instead of the trash can.

You've made your list and checked it twice, so-to-speak. It's the perfect list. Now it's time to write. Define your objectives before you start writing. Stay focused and hit the points of your objective. If you get off track, your reader is going to stop reading. Spend a lot of time on your headline. Just remember how you feel when reading mail that comes to you. After you read that headline, do you keep reading? The headline can make or break your direct mail campaign.

Does price really matter? Not unless you know what you're getting for that price. Hook your reader with all of the product benefits. By the time they get to the end, they should be saying, "I can't live without that!" And then you let them in on the price. Even if the price is extremely low, you have to tell potential customers about the product first. Disclosing this price shouldn't put people into shock. Is your product priced according to the market? If you're selling a new teddy bear, it should be priced within reason. Not many people will pay $90 for a tiny teddy bear, right? Truth is, a lot of direct mail goes unanswered because the products are unreasonably priced.

6.4. PITFALLS OF E-MAIL

These days most people who sell for a living spend 80% of their time trying to communicate with prospects via e-mail instead of actually picking up the phone and speaking with them. These days most people who sell for a living spend 80% of their time trying to communicate with prospects via e-mail instead of actually picking up the phone and speaking with them. Are you one of those people? If so, you aren't alone...but do you understand why you've turned to e-mail instead of personal contact? There are two core reasons that underlie this unfortunate trend:

1. *Fear of rejection*: The sheer negative force of anticipating rejection makes people turn to e-mail to generate new prospect relationships because it hurts less to not get a reply than to hear that verbal "no."
2. *Getting blocked by gatekeepers and voicemail*: When salespeople don't know how to break through the barriers of gatekeepers and voicemail, they start thinking, "Forget it — it's not worth the aggravation, and it takes too much energy. I'll just e-mail instead."

However, when you try to use e-mail to offer your product or service to someone who doesn't know you, you can't possibly establish the natural dialogue between two people that allows the trust level to reach the level necessary for a healthy, long-term relationship. We all know how much everyone hates e-mail spam, but even so, many salespeople are still sending introductory e-mails to decision makers. They feel that, because they're from a credible organization, they won't be associated with the negative image of a spam solicitor.

However, these introductory e-mails typically contain the traditional three-part sales pitch the introduction, a mini-presentation about the products and services being offered, and a call to action and this traditional selling approach instantly tells the recipient of the e-mail that your only goal is to sell your product or service so you can attain your goals, and not theirs.

If you're still using email to sell, watch out for these 7 pitfalls:

1. *Avoid sales pitches.* If you feel you must use e-mail to start a new relationship, make your message about issues and problems that you believe your prospects are having, but don't say anything to indicate that you're assuming that both of you are a match.

2. *Stop thinking that e-mail is the best way to get to decision makers*. Traditional selling has become so ineffective that salespeople have run out of options for creating conversation, both over the phone and in person. However, it's best to view e-mail as a backup option only, not as a way to create new relationships. Try to use it primarily for sending information and documents after you've developed a relationship with a prospect.

3. *Remove your company name from the subject line.* Whenever you put your company and solution first, you create the impression that you can't wait to give a presentation about your product and services. Your subject line should be a humble

reference to issues that you may be able to help prospects solve.

4. *Stop conditioning your prospects to hide behind e-mail.* When you e-mail prospects, it's easy for them to avoid you by not responding. Also, they get used to never picking up the phone and having a conversation with you and they may want to avoid you because they're afraid that, if they show interest in what you have to offer, you'll try to close them. This creates sales pressure the root of all selling woes. This avoidance becomes a vicious circle. If you learn to create pressure-free conversations, you'll find that you'll start getting phone calls from prospects who aren't afraid to call you.
5. Avoid using e-mail as a crutch for handling sticky sales situations.
6. *Avoid using "I" and "we."* When you start an introductory e-mail with "I" or "we," you immediately give the impression that you care only about selling your solution, rather than being open to a conversation that may or may not lead to a mutually beneficial match between what you have to offer and the issues your prospect may be trying to solve. If you can change your sales language to a natural conversation, your prospect will be less likely to stereotype your message as a spam solicitation.
7. *If you can, stop using e-mail selling altogether.* There is a way to renew your confidence and eliminate your reluctance to picking up the phone and have pleasant conversations with potential prospects. Learn a completely new way of working with gatekeepers that will get you past voicemail and to your decision makers without the rejection and

frustration that are inevitable with traditional selling approaches.

For all these reasons, you should think of e-mail as your last resort. If you can learn to pick up the phone without fear, start a trusting conversation with a gatekeeper, learn how to go beyond voice mail and find your decision makers, you'll join the thousands of people who have made the breakthrough to the most natural and efficient way of generating sales opportunities. The latest electronic databases and slice-and-dice psychographics have transformed old-fashioned direct-mail methods. With appropriate lists and laser-targeted customers, direct mail is very effective. Its reach and credibility yields results that differ from other marketing efforts.

7
HOW TO SELL VIA INTERNET

7.1. TRADITIONAL RETAILING

Retailing has become a science of controlling the consumer's movement and attention. The store has become a medium as well as a market. Stores have become a contradictory mixture of the virtual and atomic domains. What are displayed on store shelves are not the products themselves but the branded illustrated packages which we accept on faith contain the products they represent. Hence the name packaged goods. But even the products in the package are not those that we see in the brand advertising.

The hot steaming coffee which a wide-awake family is drinking at breakfast is not in the box. Open the package and you will find only the atoms of ground coffee inside. The happy family lives in the virtual world of advertising. Nor are clean clothes to be found in the box of laundry detergent. They too, and the family who wears them, only inhabit the advertising. So what's going on here? The physical, actual, atomic store is really stocking and selling virtual brands.

Consumers have to make the connection between the stuff in the boxes and cans and the brands — if they can. Such stores are rapidly becoming cemeteries of products which only come alive in advertising or in use. When you shop in these retail graveyards, you are expected to remember the living when you visit the dead. And because such stores subtract rather than add value to products, they are currently struggling to maintain profit margins of one to two percent.

7.2. MULTI-CHANNEL MARKETING

Single channel marketing must become multi-channel. Historically, most marketers have sent their goods to market through only one channel. They sold direct or though specialised intermediaries. They used either retail stores, door-to-door selling, or mail order. Groceries through grocery stores, automobiles through franchised dealers, drugs through drug stores, home furnishings, clothing, cosmetics through department stores. Travel through travel agents. Electronics through electronics stores. Books through book stores. Records through record shops. Videos through video stores etc.

Retailers and wholesalers staked their claims to lines of products, and the manufacturers were stuck with their choices. Channel conflict became a dirty word and woe to the manufacturer who tried to escape the noose. That will change as consumers demand to buy products and services at outlets of their choice. Products and services will have to be sold through multiple channels wherever and however it is least expensive and most convenient for the consumer to buy them.

7.3. DISINTERMEDIATION

Companies will eliminate layers of intermediaries. The first Industrial Revolution created mass production and new layers of distribution and communication intermediaries. The second created white collar workers and hierarchical layers of management. Both resulted in the institutional loss of information, service, relevance and dialogue. Disintermediation is already happening and it is increasing profit margins, reducing prices and providing consumers with more information and service. The virtual factory, warehouse or store, can be global, open twenty-four hours a day, seven days a week, even where local laws forbid it. Converting homes to workplaces and shopping centres are surely ideas whose time has come, even if the technology is still a work in progress.

7.4. ONE-TO-ONE MARKETING

When we talk about relationship marketing, who is to relate to whom and why? Creating a relationship is hard and sensitive work not to be left to amateurs. Too many companies trying to do relationship marketing are creating stillborn or malformed relationships. Failed or botched relationships are worse than none at all. Most people have all the relationships they need and will enter into new ones only if and when there is a clear advantage to doing so.

Business-to-business sales on the Web have been a bonanza for the likes of Dell Computers, Cisco Systems, and Gateway. They manufacture only to order and according to customer specifications. There is a complete exchange of information before and after the sale. No inventory of finished products is warehoused. Relationships are built into the transactional system and not artificially created. They are a model for the companies of the future which will bring the concepts of mass customisation and distintermediation to life.

7.5. VIRTUAL STORE

Now look at the retail marketplace. The virtual store is on its way. Such stores will pay little rent and have fewer employees and no inventory. They will basically be information-processing centres. The virtual retailer, freed of the costs of physical inventory, high rent and the danger of over-stocking too many of the wrong things, can concentrate on the business of providing service. If we supply the information, the virtual store will be able to know what each of us wants and when we want it. Thus, the virtual store can literally become a storehouse of information. It will be able to do almost anything we ask of it.

And the most important part of that sentence are the words "we ask of it." We will be able to publish our needs. We will be able to locate primary sources and choose intermediaries only if they provide a necessary service. It is our needs which will become salient, and it is we who will be able to advertise them. Each of us will become a brand and each of our brands will be unique.

The problem is not selling or delivering. It's receiving! It's about time that the Postal Service and other well-advertised deliverers realised that their improved delivery systems have already outstripped our home receiving systems. The current small post box is left over from earlier times when a paper letter in an envelope was all that a household had to receive. The Postal Service, UPS, FedEx and others ought to realise that their capacity to deliver is limited by consumers ability to receive. How long will it be before storage units for receipt of packaged goods, perishables, produce, frozen foods and hot prepared meals are part of apartment buildings, and private homes.

It only takes an architect to design them, a builder to supply them and an entrepreneur to finance them. It will happen. You can bet on it. So what of the malls, the shopping centres, and the retail stores? They may continue to exist, but not too many years hence, they won't be absolutely necessary. Two major changes will occur — they will become experiential and communal. People will leave home to seek entertainment and the society of others. Shopping will become again the social experience it once was. If all we need is a check-out counter, we won't have to go out to find it.

7.6. IMPACT OF INTERNET MARKETING

The important change is caused by the information explosion. As people try to run harder to handle their jobs, they are inundated with information from a multitude of sources. Some of it is unasked for and is found objectionable. It may be direct mail packages, telemarketing sales representatives, or unwanted e-mail (spam). A tiny fraction of this may be useful but the vast majority is an unwelcome intrusion.

Even prior to this information explosion, direct selling had been getting tougher. As markets become more international, another group of sales agents came into the market place. Many companies use Manufacturers' Representatives to be their selling force in new markets. There are few barriers to entry to such Representatives entering markets so the numbers can rise quickly.

The new element was that the sales person no longer was in control of the process. The purchaser decided if and when a potential supplier might be contacted. How could a sales person take back control? Well as it turned out, that was the wrong question. The sales person did not need to fight to regain control: that was a battle often already lost. A new phenomenon was coming into play.

If 'Push Selling' is becoming less and less effective, then perhaps it's time to switch to what might be called 'Pull Purchasing'. Purchasers are out there looking for suppliers. How can we make sure that our company will appear on their radar screens? That's where Internet Marketing comes in. Of course if you view your company website as an electronic version of your sales brochure, then you're missing most of the potential of the Internet. Your website can indeed function like an electronic sales brochure, if that's all you want.

A potential customer is interested so instead of snail-mailing a package of brochures, you direct the prospect to look at your website. It can be much more effective than the printed sales brochure. It's modern and the prospect can select exactly what they want to see. What more could you ask? To see exactly what's happening here, it should be noted that using your website as an electronic sales brochure is exactly like sending the client a CD of the website. The Internet was involved but only as the vehicle to get the content from your hosting site on to the prospect's computer.

One fundamental aspect of the Internet is that it allows A and B, who were unaware of each other's existence, to become aware and make contact. That happens between individuals and between companies millions of times each day. It's not limited by geography. A Canadian supplier can become aware of a New Zealand prospect seeking a solution just as easily as learning about a prospect in the same city. This is a growing phenomenon. Dependent on the way you measure it, the growth is at least of the order of 10 - 20% per year or possibly more. So it is increasingly important to be part of this process - "to be in the loop". Internet Marketing is the activity that ensures this.

As prospects are looking for suppliers, your company must come up in their searches. This breaks down into a two-step process. Firstly the company website must be highly visible on the Internet. One way is to ensure credible market authorities have links to the company website. So the company website should be listed in appropriate Internet trade directories. If there are prestigious Trade Shows, it may be appropriate to exhibit so that again website links are created. If there are Associations where suppliers can post links to their websites, this again can increase the company's Internet presence. All these different links from other websites are known as 'backlinks'. By one or other of these 'backlink' routes, some prospects will find the company website and start exploring the company's capabilities.

Other prospects will be following a different route. By tapping in appropriate keywords in a search engine such as Google, Yahoo! or MSN, they will hope to get a list of potential suppliers. If the company website has a good number of backlinks and has also been constructed to score well with these keywords, then the company website is likely to be listed early in this keyword listing. Such a keyword listing is usually known as a SERP (Search Engine Report Page). In very competitive market sectors, it may prove difficult to get listed highly in the SERP's. It is also possible to buy ads on these SERP's by what is known as PPC campaigns. Payments for such ads are only determined by those searchers who click on the ads and view the underlying web page. So this is a highly targeted advertising expenditure.

The Google Adwords programme and Overture are the two major players here. This first step of getting prospects to the company web page is only part of the Internet Marketing activity. The website should be constructed so that as many as possible of the visitors "convert" and move forward on the buying process. This requires that the Usability of the website be high. In other words, visitors should find it easy to get the information they are looking for. They should not get frustrated or confused by what they see in the web page. The website should also be confirming the Credibility of the company. The aim is to have these prospects contact the company and start a purchasing process. They will only do this, if all the vibes they get from the website suggest they will be satisfied with their intended purchase.

With traditional marketing activities, effectiveness is difficult to measure. This is not at all the case with Internet Marketing. Every action on the part of an Internet visitor can be measured if one wishes. So it is possible to try alternate ways of presenting information and seeing which produces the best results. The only challenges are those of handling all the information that can be developed and then of analysing it to learn what works.

So a prospect may have gone to check out the website. There are still further tasks that our Internet Marketing can do to help with that. You want to start a process of dialogue with the potential prospect. Perhaps you have some useful information that you can provide by e-mail in return for the prospect giving you some simple registration information. If appropriate, a quarterly Newsletter may help to build up a relationship of mutual respect. The prospect has needs, and you as the potential supplier have solutions. Note that none of this as yet involves the higher-priced direct selling force. The Internet Marketing staff can be doing the functions that the article described. Only when the prospect has been "qualified" should this be passed on to the direct sales force.

7.7. HOW TO START SELLING ON THE INTERNET

Creating your own product and selling on the Internet is the ideal work at home opportunity to make money online:

1. Low start-up investment.
2. Low promotion costs.
3. Simple to automate.
4. Worldwide customers.

7.8. HOW TO FIND THINGS TO SELL ON THE INTERNET

The main factor to narrow down your options is whether to sell hard goods — tangible products, or digital goods — intangible products like e-books, computer programmes and website content. The first option may be good for you if you already have an offline store and existing inventory, but, in most cases, selling digital products on the Internet is the best work at home opportunity to make money online, since these products:

1. Are relatively easy to create and very cheap to produce?
2. Can be instantly delivered by digital download — no dealing with stocking, packaging, shipping, and the like?
3. Are more suitable to purchase via the internet than via traditional offline stores?
4. Enable you to fully automate your business.

There is only one problem. In order to sell your own digital products, you must be able to create them. But, the good news is you don't have to be a talented software developer or writer. There are many resources to help you create information to sell on the Internet in the form of e-books and paid membership sites, even if you don't have any particular writing skills.

7.9. HOW TO CREATE AN ONLINE STORE

Most e-merchants dive into the process of selling on the Internet backwards. They create an online store first, and then worry about visitors. Their stores do look professional. But 9 times out of 10, there's nobody home. Nobody's browsing. Nobody's searching. And most importantly, nobody's buying. And 98% die and give up within a year. Why?

Merchant Mistake - create an online store, Then worry about traffic. Open a storefront on a busy "real world" street - visitors will spill in and buy. Selling on the Internet, however, doesn't work like that. People aren't looking for you... they are looking for information. The only way that your online store, or any other monetisation model, can succeed, is to follow the CTPM process: Content ® Traffic ® Presell ® Monetise. In short, it means:

— *Content.* Online, people search for information and solutions. So give them what they want by turning what you know into high-quality, in-demand content.

— *Traffic.* Your theme-based topical content ranks high at the Search Engines, attracting free, targeted traffic... interested, motivated, targeted, "open-to-you" visitors.

— *Presell.* Develop trust, credibility and confidence by overdelivering relevant, original, high-value information to these motivated, "open-to-you" pre-customers.

— *Monetise.* Convert your warm, willing-to-buy visitors into revenue, in various ways. Sell hard goods, e-goods, your personal or professional services. Or earn income without selling at all, through Google Ads, affiliate fees, finder's fees, etc.

There are plenty of tools on the Net that can help you create an online store - a quick visit to Amazon Zshops, eBay Marketplace, or Yahoo! Stores will confirm this. But, there is only one product in the world that takes you step-by-step through the powerful, natural CTPM process - Site Build It (SBI). SBI is the most comprehensive and well established product among other small business website builders. You won't find any other tool that can show results like this. However, until recently, SBI didn't include an integrated shopping cart or online store functionality (it's fully compatible with many plug-and-play third party solutions).

But now, with the launch of Store Build It (StBI), every owner of SBI site can use this new opportunity and create a highly trafficked, profitable online store. SBI and StBI are a powerful one-two combo that work together:

— *Site Build It*. This is the engine that drives targeted, credentialised, PREsold traffic to Store Build It. Traffic is the lifeblood of any online store.

— *Store Build It*. Completely integrated into SBI (it runs on a subdomain of main SBI site) StBI is a powerful and flexible world-class online store.

Obviously, Store Build It isn't available as a standalone product for the very reason that there simply cannot be "M" without "CTP" first. Build a highly trafficked website. Presell. Then, and only then, use Store Build It to create an online store and monetise.

8

HOW TO CREATE EFFECTIVE SALE PRESENTATIONS

Sales are an integral part of the business world and one of the most important tasks in a firm. However, sales can often be complicated. This chapter describes the elements involved in creating an effective sales presentation.

A sales presentation should not be scripted. It seldom follows a predictable path. Daily shifts in business needs and variations in human nature make every presentation a walk on the wire without a net. The salesman who makes it all the way to the sale is often the one with the best presentation. This includes much more than just product knowledge, and in this session we cover the full spectrum of what it takes to succeed. Many salespeople never adequately deal with a customer's objections, preferring to ignore the subject all together. Others fall back on the highly manipulative tactics that are often advocated.

When preparing for a sales presentation, the salesperson needs to think of the three V's: Visual, Vocal, and Verbal. These are communication signals that can be practiced before, and delivered during the presentation.

8.1. VISUAL PRESENTATION

Appearance is vital to the presentation. Even if the dress

code is casual for the customer, the salesperson should dress professionally. While dressing too professionally will not hurt the sale, dressing too casually may. Clothes should be conservative, well fitting, and comfortable. The salesperson's appearance should not detract from the presentation. Facial expressions can relay a lot of information to the customer about the salesperson throughout the presentation (e.g., confidence in the product, boredom, or genuine concern for the customer). The salesperson should remember to make regular eye contact and use hand gestures to emphasise a point, but should never sway, fidget, or cross his arms.

8.2. VOCAL PRESENTATION

There are six vocal cues to remember when delivering a presentation: pitch, volume, rate, punch, pause, and diction. It is important to remember that it is not what you say, but how you say it. Practice simple vocal exercises so that your voice will remain at a steady and relaxed level in front of customers. Vocal cues are used to keep the customer interested and to prevent the salesperson from speaking in monotones. Make sure that the presentation can be easily heard, that key words are emphasised, and that the pace of the presentation is easy to follow. Practice these six vocal cues with a friend, spouse, or colleague.

8.3. VERBAL PRESENTATION

To prevent weakening the salesperson's position, keep the following points in mind: avoid long, rambling sentences (e.g., use descriptive language and short sentences), avoid using buzz words and jargon (e.g., words that only used within a specific industry), and avoid tag questions and qualifiers (e.g., "I think this is a good product, don't you?). Keep the points focused and do not use expressions such as "umm", "like", and "you know", which detract from the presentation and may cause the customer to lose focus.

8.4. PLANNING AND PREPARATION

Planning for a presentation helps the salesperson to be organised, prepared, and confident. When planning for a presentation, it is helpful to think of the presentation as having three main features: content, style, and rapport. These are necessary for a good presentation. For instance, it is of little benefit to have good content (e.g., facts to enhance the product) without style if there is no rapport between the salesperson and the customer. Similarly, it is of little use to have great style and rapport with the customer if there is no content.

8.5. ACTUAL PRESENTATION

There are many ways to make a sale, but it takes time. The salesperson should always time the presentation so that the customer never feels "rushed" into making a decision. Rushing the customer due to other time commitments will usually hurt the seller. Make sure to ask if anything has changed since the customer and salesperson last met. This will help avoid going down the wrong path in the presentation. Also, ask where the customer is in the decision-making process. This will help the salesperson determine the likeliness of making a sale that day (or scheduling another appointment for later) and whether there is other competition involved.

Try to begin the presentation with a quick review of the goals and objectives of the customer's firm. This will help focus the presentation and let the customer know that the salesperson is interested in the customer's needs. The salesperson should use visuals to gain the customer's attention and give focus to the presentation. Visuals often help to illustrate key points and help build rapport between the salesperson and customer. Be concise and factual. The customer will feel more comfortable buying from the salesperson if he feels that the salesperson is straightforward and honest.

8.6. EFFECTIVE PRESENTATION

A presentation is an opportunity for a speaker to give a rehearsed 'speech' or statement, generally without interruption in order to persuade or to influence. It can be to a group of two, or an audience of thousands. But, there are many things which can go wrong and much planning to do beforehand. If you have been doing it for years, you know the problems and plan accordingly. If you are a novice then the planning has to be really comprehensive. Here are some tips covering the main areas which make presentations successful. If you can get the equipment, the visuals, the words, the delivery and finally the environment right, then what can go wrong?

People remember around 25% of what they hear, 50% of what they see and hear, 75% of what they see, hear and say, and 100% of what they see, hear, say and do. Talks only hit 25% of recollection; using visuals can increase this to 75%. They can greatly enhance a presentation provided there are not too many with too much information! Simple visual aids should serve as the speaker's notes. The titles should be "triggers" to what you want to say next. If you know your subject well and have rehearsed your presentation, your visual aids should be all you need to "jog" your memory.

Visual aids allow you to move around the room. You may not want to move around, but movement helps you to relax and adds energy to your presentation. Movement also allows the listeners to follow you and pay close attention to you. You can also have good eye contact with your audience all the time, except when you look briefly at your visual aid when audience will also look at the visual. This will help them see, as well as hear, your message.

1. You or the screen. Have a small table for notes or to stack slides before and after you use them.
2. Place your screen on a diagonal to the audience instead of directly behind you. This will ensure that you do not block the view for your audience. Also, have the top of the screen tilted forward towards the overhead projector (if possible) to prevent the "keystone" effect (this is where the top of the image is larger than the bottom).
3. Label and very clearly number each slide. Write their number or name in the margin of your notes as well. This will help you keep your presentation organised, and in sequence as you present it. It will also aid the transition from one topic to the next by telling you what's coming up next.
4. When projecting, cover the transparency with an opaque piece of paper. You can see what is coming next before revealing it to the audience. You should also turn the projector off between slides.

8.6.1 Computer Presentations

The popularity of computers to generate presentations is growing. Laptop computers with common software packages such as PowerPoint, are coupled to a digital (electronic) projector or "light box" as it is often known. Highly professional and entertaining presentations can be given using this exciting technology. However, the equipment is expensive and you need to know how to work it. Many hotels need to hire in projectors at half day, or full day rates. The cost of bulbs is expensive. The units themselves are small and lightweight.

1. Read the projector manual thoroughly. Not all projectors work in the same way and each has its own unique operating requirements. Become very familiar with the projector before using it in your actual presentation. Make sure your computer can be properly interfaced.
2. Spend some time making sure you know how to set up the projector with your computer and other computers. If possible, set up the projector in the actual presentation environment you will be using.
3. Projector bulbs have a limited life, some shorter than others. Check and make sure the bulb is not close to the end of its life and know where there is a spare.
4. Check out the actual presentation for the colours you will be using. Some colours and colour combinations do not project well. Use dark backgrounds for this medium. Check the spelling on screen where mistakes look bigger and are more noticeable than on a PC screen. Check that words can be read from the back of a room, if they can't, increase the font size or make them bold.
5. Handouts can be produced from the slides and you can easily insert your name and contact details so delegates can contact you later. You can also print out you own notes as part of the handout.

8.6.2 Flip Charts

Although many presenters prefer to use high-tech computer generated presentations, the flip chart still continues to be an effective presentation medium. It is easy to use, cheap, can be interactive with the audience, is reliable and ideal for small numbers. The purpose of using visual aids is to enhance your presentation not upstage it, so there are still many good reasons to use flip charts.

1. The best flip chart stands have clamps or holes at the top and will hold most type of flip chart pads. Find out what sort of flip chart stand you will be using beforehand.
2. Pads come either plain or with grid lines on them. Grid lines makes your job easier in drawing straight lines and keeping the text aligned. Make sure the pad has perforations at the top to allow easier removal of sheets. You can now get "Post-It" flip charts which enable you to stick torn off sheets around a room.
3. Design your charts on paper first before drawing them on the actual flip chart pad.
4. Lightly write the text in pencil first before using the actual flip chart markers. This allows you to make any adjustments with text spacing and any figures you will be drawing. Using upper and lower case letters makes it easier to read. Use the 7 x 7 rule - have no more than 7 words on each line and no more than 7 lines to a sheet. But 6 x 6 is better!
5. Use flip chart markers and not 'magic markers'. Flip chart markers will not "bleed" through the paper and do not have as strong a smell as regular markers. You can also find "fruit scented" markers on sale!
6. Avoid using the colours yellow, pink, or orange which are extremely difficult for the audience to see. Use one dark colour and one accent colour for maximum impact.

7. Write any notes you need next to key points, in pencil. The audience won't be able to see them. It is a good idea to also write what is on the next sheet so that you can introduce the topic before turning over.
8. Have a blank sheet of paper between each of your text sheets. This will prevent the written material from other sheets to "peek" through.
9. Store and transport your flip charts in a case or the cardboard box that it came in to protect and keep them fresh and ready to use each time.
10. Making "prepared" flip charts can take a considerable amount of time. Make sure you start preparing early enough so you can review them and make any changes or corrections in advance.

8.6.3 Tips for Making Good Visuals

Following are few points for good visuals:

1. Use readable fonts, preferable one type only and stay away from the fancy stuff.
2. Keep to one or two major points per visual and use one line 'sentences'.
3. Limit to around five points (lines) per visual
4. Use simple graphics, diagrams, pictures, clip arts and graphs.
5. Use colour to differentiate between visuals
6. Make sure that OHP slides have a light background, PC generated slides, dark.
7. Don't use too many visuals, about 1 per 2 minutes. And beware "Death by PowerPoint", entertain, don't confuse with whizzy graphics and technology!

8.6.4. How to Prepare an Effective Text of a Talk

There are several ways to prepare the text of a talk, writing it out in full, jotting notes, preparing a 'mind map' or simply turning up and doing it 'off-the-cuff'. Most people write their text in full, memorise the salient points, transfer these to postcard sized notes (held together by a piece of string) and keep the full text to one side just in case they forget their speech. Whatever method, it has got to be right for you, for the presentation and the time to be taken.

If you type out your notes in full and read them out loud, add 50% to the time to give you an idea of the length of your talk. People have a short attention span. Generally 45 minutes is the limit, then there is a distinct dip in concentration for 5 minutes, before another 45 minute session. Giving the audience a 'structure' will help them follow your talk and also prevent you wandering!

8.6.4.1. The introduction

1. Thank the audience for the invitation to speak to them,
2. Tell them who you are (establish your credentials),
3. Tell them how long the presentation will last,
4. Outline what you hope to achieve by the end of that time,
5. Explain if notes will be given out, or if they should take them,
6. Invite questions during, or at the end of the talk.

This part can be summarised by "tell 'em what you are going to tell 'em, then tell 'em, then tell 'em what you've told 'em!" That means giving the audience a Beginning, a Middle and an End.

8.6.4.2. *The beginning*

In your presentation you are trying to ensure that the audience remember 75% of your talk, by seeing, hearing and participating. Identifying a problem they may have will grab their attention at the outset. You can do this by :

1. Asking a direct question and waiting for an answer (How do you feel about that?).
2. Asking an indirect question (How do you think people feel about that?).
3. Making a statement (The main problem with ....).
4. Telling a story (Recently I spoke to ... who said that....).

In this section you are considering the audience's needs — anticipating their problems is often the easiest way of focusing attention on your topic. In a small group, asking open questions is simplest — questions beginning with who, what, why, how, when and where?. This may lead to open discussion, however, and deflect you from your prepared talk, so use with caution! With larger groups a statement can be made using the third party, followed by a question or series of three questions like, "Many people find it difficult to keep up with changes in technology. Do you find that?"

If you have asked direct questions of your audience and got replies then you can you summarise with words like "Based on what you have said, it seems that your main problems are .... and...... Is this correct?" This will then allow you to go back to your prepared text, slides, flip chart or notes. You now have their attention and involvement and can then move on to the presentation of solutions to their problems.

8.6.4.3. The middle

Tell them what your solution, idea, concept etc. means:

1. In terms that they can understand
2. Give them the facts about your product, service, idea or argument. Show them how it works, and how it will work for them.
3. Show how they can solve their problems by identifying the problem and various solutions before stressing your own solution.
4. Try not to use jargon or technical terms unless you are certain the listener can understand.

Even for a very large audience, a question like "Is that clear?" or "Do you find that?" can gauge the level of attention as well as clarifying that you are on the right track.

1. Anticipate their questions or objections to your ideas.
2. Make assumptions about the thoughts of the listener ("You may be saying to yourself, how much will this cost?") before moving on to the next visual which gives the answer.
3. Use third party objections/questions ("I am often asked why the cost is so low compared to ....")
4. For small groups, ask for specific question. Anticipate their questions – delivery, price, discounts, terms, contracts etc. Anticipate their reasons for rejecting your argument, idea, product or aim.

8.6.4.4. The end

If you have answered all questions to the satisfaction of the listener, you can now assume the sale or the acceptance of your proposition. So the final part is to close.

1. Summarise the problems the audience faces, the solutions you are proposing, the facts about you product or service and the answers to questions posed, or imagined.
2. Then tell them what happens next, how they can 'buy' or what you will do for the listener. Ask for their business. Tell them what to do if they have any further questions or want clarification.
3. Thank them for their close attention and for giving you their time. Tell them you are grateful. Hand out any notes which may be available.

8.6.5. Right Delivery of Your Presentation

Making any presentation, even for experts, is a nerve wracking task. You will, and should, be nervous, but remember the audience is there to listen to you. They want to be there. You should have rehearsed and rehearsed so that you are word perfect. All you need now is to speak with confidence and conviction.

Standing comfortably: Many presenters like to sit to make their presentation. However, the more nervous they are, the lower they slip down in a chair. A table acts as a barrier between you and the audience — a barrier to your message as well! And there is always a temptation to bang the desk, literally. Standing gives you more authority and generally places you above your audience. It enables you to keep your head high and opens the throat enabling you to project your voice well. Stand with you legs slightly apart, put notes on a lectern or hold them in your hand. Make sure notes are secured so that, if you drop them, they won't scatter all over the floor.

Breathing properly: Breathing starts from the diaphragm. Take a few deep breaths before you start talking, it helps to settle the nerves. Take a long deep breath and count out loud, slowly, until you run out of breath - you should be able to get to fifteen or twenty without straining the vocal chords. Don't take a lot of fast deep breaths if you are particularly tense, you will pass out! If you are relaxed, you may only take 4 or 5 breaths per minute, sometimes even less.

Exercising beforehand: Simply flexing the toes, shaking the arms and legs, nodding your head and rotating the shoulders will ease tension and help with nerves. It will relax the body and let the mind and mouth concentrate on the job in hand.

Modulating the voice: If you listen to newsreaders, you will detect the rise and fall of the voice according the message being put over. This helps to retain interest and keep attention. But there are other methods :

1. Increase the level of the voice to 'wake up' the audience or emphasise a phrase.
2. Speak quietly to emphasise confidentiality or let people into a secret.
3. Stress individual words, leaving a space between each one to indicate an emotion like annoyance, importance, encouragement, passion or anger.
4. Speak faster to indicate a lesser importance to the text.

Accent: Many people worry about their accent. They shouldn't. You must be natural. Speak slowly, the larger the audience the slower you must speak. The slower you speak, the better the enunciation of each word and, therefore, the less any accent shows through.

8.6.6. Tips for Making Right Environment

Very often you do not know where you are going to give a presentation. It could be an office, lecture theatre, conference room or hotel. This puts you at a disadvantage so if you can go to a venue early, it will help a great deal. The good presenters turn up in the morning for an afternoon session, say, so that they can become fully familiar with the surroundings, how the voice carries, what noise they must compete with and so on. This 'environment' can be the make or break of a presentation. It is the only presentational area you cannot control. It is the only presentational area you cannot control. So here are a few tips:

1. Take emergency supplies with you including markers, name tags/place cards, extension leads and parcel tape, spare bulbs, fuses and gloves to change hot bulbs. Write out a page of notes of other things to take with you like slides, floppy disc, blue-tak, drawing pins, notes, headache pills and so on.
2. Liase in advance with the organisers and check everything you have direct control over, handouts, flip charts, overheads, Audio/Visual support equipment and slides. Leave nothing unchecked.
3. Make sure there are no distractions for the audience. Think about room temperature, extraneous noises, distracting pictures, sunshine in delegates eyes or on your screen and standing in front of a picture window.
4. Arrive early and check out facilities. Make sure that all the equipment works and is in the correct position.
5. Decide on the room layout to suit your presentation and style. Main layouts are classroom, theatre style or in a horseshoe.

8.7. EASIEST WAYS TO BLOW A SALES PRESENTATION

Following are some easiest ways to blow a sales presentation.

1. *Use the same presentation over and over*: Your presentation worked well once, (actually only once and that was last year), but you should stick with it. Don't let the fact that your sales cycle is 2 months longer lead you to think customising your initial presentation is valuable time spent.
2. *Edit critical marketing messages you don't like*: Sure, millions of pounds has been invested in branding. And it may be that the integrated messaging is what got the client to ask for a face-to-face presentation. But if you don't like it, chances are your client doesn't either.
3. *Spend hours searching for key slides*: It is vitally important to hunt for phantom slides that you saw someone use at some point during some meeting for some client. The more time you search, the closer you are to closing the deal. And just think how relaxed you'll be.
4. *Send frantic emails begging for updated content*: The night before the big meeting is the perfect time to email blast the product manager, sales support team, and fellow reps for the slides presented at the national sales meeting. Ignore any response that says you should have them on a CD sent to you last month. What CD?
5. *Avoid presenting new product offerings*: If you don't know everything about a product, don't present it. Don't even mention it. Stick with what you know. If the client asks about it, the marketing manager can fly in for that part of the presentation. Cross selling is not for the faint of heart.

6. *Show outdated presentation content*: Financials, industry trends, statistics — all are outdated the minute they are released. So, show what you've got even if it is your company web site, collateral material, and sales sheets that don't have the most up-to-date information.
7. *Make up the customer testimonial*: Don't let reality interfere with creativity. Draft a case study or quote that portrays what the experience would be like if everything went well. If the prospect wants to talk to the customer, well...we'll cross that bridge when we come to it.
8. *Delete any required legal or regulatory slide*: IFA, SEC, regulatory commissions, and legal departments get very cranky about disclaimers. The fact that they are there to protect everyone involved should not dissuade you from removing them.
9. *Don't listen to the audience*: Once you begin a presentation, don't let the client interrupt. If they ask questions, tell them to hold them to the end. You need time to prove how smart you are.
10. *Never share a sales presentation that works*: If, by chance, you come across a slide or a series of slides that was particularly effective, do not let other reps or marketing people know about it. That way, your sales will increase even if overall revenue growth does not.

9

HOW TO MAKE IT EASY FOR CUSTOMER TO BUY FROM YOU

Sales performance is the lifeblood of every business. Whether you are an account manager, a field sales representative, or less obviously a customer services agent, one of your key goals is to sell your products, services and ideas.

However things have become far too complex. In a world where companies are striving to come up with the next product or service that will make our lives easier, the very process that is used to sell these latest products or services is becoming ever more complicated. It's time to go back to making it easier for your customers to buy from you.

The key principles of how to make it easy for people to buy from will not necessarily be new to you - building trust and a good relationship for example, as well as understanding what your customer really wants, are fundamental to sales success. Including five key principles to show you how to optimise your product:

1. How to create and maintain a Valuable Customer Relationship.
2. Establishing what is Valuable to the Customer.
3. Providing what is valuable to the customer.

4. Gaining a Commitment to Action.
5. Creating a well-formed sales goal.

9.1. WAYS TO IMPROVE YOUR SALES

Here are four easy ways you can boost your sales for little or no new expense and without making major changes in your selling process.

1. *Focus on What Your Customers Really Want*: Your customers really don't want your products or services. They don't even want what those products or services do for them. What they really want is to gain the specific feeling they get after buying and using your products or services. Emphasise the feelings produced by using your product instead of talking about what your product is -or how it works. For example, if you sell financial products, describe what it feels like to enjoy an affluent life style without debt.
2. *Keep Communicating With Your Previous Non-Buyers*: You've heard it before — but I'll say it here again. Most prospective customers will not buy the first time they see or hear about your product or service. You're losing a lot of sales if you do not persistently follow up with those prospects. Your follow up procedure can be as simple as periodically contacting them with a new offer. Or it can be more complex like distributing a newsletter or providing updated product information. Example, offer a special report, a list of sources or some other valuable information your prospects cannot get anywhere else. Deliver it only by email or postal mail so you can get their contact address.
3. *Encourage Questions*: Questions from prospects may be a nuisance. But answering them can be very

profitable. Prospective customers only take time to ask questions when they have a high level of interest in your product or service. Providing a satisfactory answer to a prospect's question often leads directly to a sale. Invite prospects to ask questions when in live selling situations. And make it easy for them to ask questions when they are not such as at your web site. For example, list a phone number or email address where you or someone else can answer their questions.

4. *Make Buying Easier*: Every non-essential action in the buying process is an opportunity for the customer to reverse their decision causing you to lose the sale.

These four selling tactics may not be new to you. But are you using all (or any) of them? If not, they can easily boost your sales for little or no new expense — and without making major changes in your sales process.

9.2. MAKING SALES IS EASY

Friends buy from friends. Because people trust that their friends will go above and beyond the duties of a typical salesperson. They know that their friends will give them friendly, honest help and provide them with the product that is perfect for their needs. In return, these people develop into loyal customers who are happy to support their friend's business with continued sales and referrals.

So how do you take advantage of this wonderful sales cycle? You must change the focus of the sales experience on making a friend rather than making a sale. When you focus on making a friend at all costs, you will find ways to serve your customers beyond the scope of what you do in your business. This type of exceptional service is what will get your customers talking positively about you after the fact. They will enthusiastically tell everybody they know about you, your company and your excellent service. These testimonials are the most effective form of advertising you could ever have for your company. By making one friend, you will create customer loyalty that will boost your sales as they continue to buy from you and recommend you to others. In order to be friends with your customers, you must take the time to revaluate several key aspects of how you interact with them.

Your customers do you a great service by contacting you. Think about it. If a customer contacts you or stops into your place of business, they have already paid you a wonderful compliment. They likely have heard that you do good business or that you have the solution to their problem. Return that compliment by respecting your customers and letting them know that you are honoured that they have given you the opportunity to earn their business. Recognising the important value of each customer will establish the loyalty that will keep your friendships and sales numbers growing.

The only way to become friends with your customers is by caring about them as a friend would. You must listen to your customer's concerns and understand the meaning behind their words. Everything from your tone to the product that you recommend for them should reflect your sincere desire to make them happy and to solve the problem that they brought to you. Because this type of attention and service is so rare in business today, you will create relationships with your customers that are just as rare. This unique relationship will be the driving force behind their purchases.

Your customers come to you because they need help and they trust that you will be able to supply them with the information they need. Do not take advantage of that vulnerability and belittle their intelligence while speaking with them. Avoid phrases that may sound condescending. After all, knowing every intricate detail of your product is your job, not theirs. Your mockery and disrespect will be evident to your customer, and will be sure to end the possibility of their friendship and business.

Treating your customer like a friend also means letting go of many of the techniques typical salespeople may use. Do not fall into the trap of trying a manipulative sales trick on your customer. You do not like it when it is done to you, so do not do it to your customer. If you are focused on your customers needs, there will be no need for finding a manipulative way to close the sale.

Employing manipulative sales processes and formulaic closing techniques insults your customer's intelligence and paints you in a shadowy light. This is obviously not good when it comes to earning their trust, their respect, and, most importantly, their business. Making friends with your customers is an easy way to ensure a sales experience where everybody wins. Your customers will feel confident buying from a friendly and trustworthy business, and you will enjoy the benefits of new friendships and continued sales.

9.3 ONLINE PAYMENTS SYSTEM

The process of credit card enabling your brick-and-mortar business. Accepting credit cards can help increase revenue and speed up cash flow. You will need the following to accept credit cards on your website:

1. An electronic shopping cart system;
2. A payment gateway service;
3. A credit card processor; and
4. An internet merchant account issued by a bank or other financial institution or service bureau.

Here's how online credit card processing works.

1. Your customer submits his credit card information at checkout on your website.
2. The shopping cart software sends the transaction to the gateway.
3. The gateway routes the information to the processor.
4. The processor contacts the bank that issued the customer's credit card.
5. The issuing bank approves or declines the transaction.
6. The processor routes the result back to the gateway who then passes the result back to the website shopping cart system. The entire process is done electronically and takes seconds to complete.

Here's a quick refresher for those who missed the basics, then we'll talk about the shopping cart system you'll need to implement on your website.

Payment Gateway Service: The payment gateway service comes into play when a customer submits their credit card information to the webpage form. Think of the gateway service as the middleman in the process. The website's shopping cart checkout system electronically submits the credit card to the gateway service that then routes the information to the processor for approval.

Credit Card Processor: The credit card processor is an electronic data centre that processes the credit card transactions coming from the gateway company, ensures that the charge is valid, then settles the funds in your merchant account.

Internet Merchant Account: An Internet merchant account is a bank or account in which funds from online sales are deposited by the processor. Merchant accounts are usually issued by banks that are associated with the major credit card services like Visa and MasterCard. Be aware that many banks will not grant merchant accounts to Internet merchants as they are often categorised as "high risk ventures." This policy varies widely and in the end, the granting of the merchant account will come down to economics from the bank's point of view. If the bank sees even the smallest iota of risk, you will not be granted the account.

Fortunately, the growth of online sales has given rise to an entire industry of merchant service bureaus that will grant you a merchant account and everything else you need to accept online payments. The fees are usually higher, but it's better than not having an online payment system at all.

9.4. SHOPPING CART SYSTEM

To accept online payments you must have what's called a "shopping cart system" that allows the customer to select and purchase products from your website. A shopping cart system typically consists of three components: the product catalogue, the shopping cart, and the checkout/payment system. The product catalogue is the component that displays the items you have for sale on the website. The shopping cart system is the component that allows your customers to select products by clicking to "add items to cart," and the checkout/payment system is the component that allows the customer to complete the checkout process and pay for their purchase with a credit card (or in some cases an electronic check). It is the checkout/payment component that communicates with the gateway system to complete the transaction.

Adding a shopping cart system to your website can be a simple or highly complex task, depending on the system you select. The cost of shopping cart software ranges from free (for simplistic form-based systems) to very expensive. Which shopping cart system is best for your business depends on a number of factors, including the product you're selling, the depth of your product line, the purchase options you wish to offer customers, the inventory control functionality, and the extent of automation you desire. There are numerous companies who can assist in the setup of your shopping cart and online credit card payment system.

These companies typically charge several hundred to several thousand dollars for their services, but like anything you get what you pay for, so always use a company with good references in this area. When you're dealing with something as important as credit card processing and cash flow, bite the bullet and get it done right the first time. The money you spend now will be returned many times in increased sales volume from credit card customers. The most important thing to remember when setting up an online payment system is this: online it's all about security and privacy.

Though online credit card processing has been around for years there are still many people who are uncomfortable giving their credit card number online. These are the same folks who do not hesitate to give their credit card number over the phone or hand their credit card to a waiter who disappears with it for ten minutes. Online credit card processing is much less susceptible to fraud and abuse than of those scenarios.

In today's highly competitive economy, it is difficult to maintain a significant market advantage based on your professional skills alone. Developing professional relationships with your customers is key to your success. No matter what business you are in, the most powerful value-added you can contribute in any business strategy is the "trust factor". The level of confidence in corporate America is at an all-time low, and suspicion of "all things corporate" is on the rise. Customers and prospects are in search of reliability and credibility in their business dealings. Although people do business with other people they know and can rely on, building this solid foundation does not happen overnight.

Why is something as personal as trust important in a business environment? Trust can be defined as a firm belief in the honesty of another and the absence of suspicion regarding his motives or practices. The concept of trust in business dealings is simple: Build on an individual's confidence in you and eliminate fear as an operating principle. To cultivate trust, take the risk of being open with customers and prospects. This enables them to perceive you as a real person—one with strengths and weaknesses that come into play as the business relationship develops. When trust is reciprocal, you will find that your confidence in others is rewarded by their support and reinforcement of what you also stand for as a business entity.

9.5. LETTING GO OF FEAR

Let go of fear, which restricts your ability to relate to others. Letting go frees you of behavioural constraints that can immobilise your professional development. Fear of rejection, fear of failure, fear of success, fear of being hurt, fear of the unknown—all these are roadblocks to developing and growing a trusting relationship with your customers. Let go of your fear of losing an account or not having the right answers. Leave all your fears at the customer's or prospect's doorstep. Other critical steps in cultivating business trust are knowing who you are and knowing your potential value to your customers.

The interaction that results from this can have a tremendous impact on your sales. People don't just buy from anyone. They buy from people they can trust. The rapport and credibility you establish with the trust factor go a long way toward building customer confidence in your ability to meet all of the business needs. Trust has both an active and a passive component in a business relationship. The active feeling of trust is confidence in your leadership, veracity, and reliability, based on a track record of performance. Never ignore the passive feeling of trust. This is absence of worry or suspicion may be unrecognised or taken for granted in our most productive relationships, but it is the foundation that long lasting business interactions are built on.

9.6. BUILD TRUST WITH CUSTOMERS

How do you build trust with customers? First, you need to really care about them. Obviously, your customers care about your knowledge, expertise, and accomplishments. However, they care even more about the level of concern you have for them. Successful trust-building hinges on four actions: engaging, listening, framing, and committing. The trust factor can be realised once we understand these components of trust and incorporate them in our business dealings. Engaging customers and prospects occurs when you show genuine concern and interest in their business and its problems.

Maintain good eye contact and body posture. Good eye contact signifies openness and honesty. Your body language and other forms of nonverbal communication speak volumes about your attitude toward them. By the same token, you want to be aware of eye contact and body language in your customers or potential customers. What they don't say can speak volumes! Listening with understanding and empathy is possible if you think customer focus first. Let the customer tell his story. Put yourself in his shoes when you listen to his business concerns, purpose, vision, and desires. Show approval or understanding by nodding your head and smiling during the conversation.

Separate the process of taking in information from the process of judging it. Just suspend your judgment and focus on the customer. Framing what the customer or prospect has said is the third action in trust-building. Make sure you have formed an accurate understanding of his problems and concerns. Confirm what you think you heard by asking open-ended questions such as "What do you mean by that?" or "Help me to understood the major production problems you are experiencing." After you have clarified the problems, start to frame them in order of importance. By identifying the areas in which you can help the customer, you offer her clarity in her own mind and continue to build her trust.

Committing is the final action for developing the trust factor. Communicate enthusiastically your plan of action for solving the customer's problems. Help the customer see what it will take to achieve the end result. Presumably, what you have said up to this point has been important, but what you do now—how you commit—is even more important. Remember the old adage "Action speaks louder than words." Show you want this customer's business long term. Complete assignments and projects on budget and on time. Then follow up with customers periodically to see how your partnership is faring.

In the final analysis, business trust stems from keeping our word. If we say we will be there for our customers, then we should honour that commitment...by being there. Trust results from putting the customer's best interest before our own, from being dependable, from being open and forthcoming with relevant information. It is impossible to overestimate the power of the trust factor in our professional lives. Truly, trust is the basis of all enduring, long-term business relationships.

Customer care involves putting systems in place to maximise your customers' satisfaction with your business. It should be a prime consideration for every business — your sales and profitability depends on keeping your customers happy. Customer care is more directly important in some roles than others. For receptionists, sales staff and other employees in customer-facing roles, customer care should be a core element of their job description and a core criterion when you're recruiting.

But don't neglect the importance of customer care in other areas of your business. For instance, your warehousing and dispatch departments may have minimal contact with your customers - but their performance when fulfilling orders has a major impact on customers' satisfaction with your business. A huge range of factors can contribute to customer satisfaction, but your customers - both consumers and other businesses - are likely to take into account:

1. How well your product or service matches customer needs.
2. The value for money you offer.
3. Your efficiency and reliability in fulfilling orders.
4. The professionalism, friendliness and expertise of your employees.
5. How well you keep your customers informed.
6. The after-sales service you provide.

For customer-facing employees such as receptionists and salespeople, customer care is a core part of the job. Customer service levels should be a key criterion when recruiting for these roles. Your existing customers are among the most important assets of your business - they have already chosen you instead of your competitors. Keeping their custom costs far less than attracting new business, so it's worth taking steps to make sure that they're satisfied with the service they receive.

There are a number of techniques you can employ, including:

1. Providing a free customer helpline.
2. Answering frequently asked questions on your website.
3. Following up sales with a courtesy call.
4. Providing free products that will help customers look after or make the most of their purchases.
5. Sending reminders when services or check-ups are due.
6. Offering preferential discounts to existing customers on further purchases.

Existing customer relationships are opportunities to increase sales because your customers will already have a degree of trust in your recommendations. Cross-selling and up-selling are ways of increasing either the range or the value of what you sell by pointing out new purchase possibilities to these customers. Alerting customers when new, upgraded or complimentary products become available — perhaps through regular emails or newsletters — is one way of increasing sales.

To retain your customers' trust, however, never try to sell them something that clearly doesn't meet their needs. Remember, your aim is to build a solid long-term relationship with your customers rather than to make quick one-off profits. Satisfied customers will contribute to your business for years, through their purchases and through recommendations and referrals of your business.

In business-to-business trading, providing a high level of customer care often requires you to find out what your customers want. Once you have identified your most valuable customers or best potential customers, you can target your highest levels of customer care towards them. Another approach, particularly in the consumer market, is the obligation to treat all consumers to the highest standard.

Information about your customers and what they want is available from many sources, including:

1. Their order history.
2. Records of their contacts with your business - phone calls, meetings and so on.
3. Direct feedback — if you ask them, customers will usually tell you what they want.
4. Changes in individual customers' order patterns.
5. Changes in the overall success of specific products or services.
6. Feedback about your existing range - what it does and doesn't do.
7. Enquiries about possible new products or services.
8. Feedback from your customers about things they buy from other businesses.
9. Changes in the goods and services your competitors are selling.
10. Feedback and referrals from other, non-competitive suppliers.

9.7. MANAGE CUSTOMER INFORMATION

It's important that you draw up a plan about how customer information is to be gathered and used in your business. Establish a customer-care policy. Assign a senior manager as the policy's champion but make sure that all your staff are involved — often the lower down the scale you go, the more contact with customers there is. You can manage your customer records using a database system or with customer relationship management software.

While good overall service is the best way of generating customer loyalty, sometimes new relationships can be strengthened, or old ones refreshed, using customer loyalty schemes. These are programmes that use fixed or percentage discounts, extra goods or prizes to reward customers for behaviour that benefits your business. They can also be used to persuade customers to give you another try if you feel you have successfully tackled past problems with your customer service. You can decide to offer rewards on the basis of:

1. Repeat custom.
2. Cumulative spend.
3. Orders for large quantities or with a high value.
4. Prompt payment.
5. Length of relationship.

For example, a car wash might offer free cleaning every tenth visit or a free product if a customer opts for the deluxe service. A mail-order company might seek to revive the interest of lapsed customers by offering a voucher redeemable against purchases - response rates with such vouchers can be improved by setting an expiry date. You can also provide key customers with loyalty cards that entitle them to a discount on all their purchases. Employees who deal with customers' orders should be fully aware of current offers and keep customers informed. Sometimes brochures and other marketing materials are the best way of getting word out about a new customer incentive. Your customers' view of the overall service you provide will influence their loyalty more than short-term rewards will.

9.8. CUSTOMER FEEDBACK AND CONTACT PROGRAMMES

Customer feedback and contact programmes are two ways of increasing communication with your customers.

They can represent great opportunities to listen to your customers and to let them know more about what you can offer. Customer feedback can provide you with detailed information about how your business is perceived. It's a chance for customers to voice objections, suggest changes or endorse your existing processes, and for you to listen to what they say and act upon it. Feedback is most often gathered using questionnaires, in person, over the telephone or by post.

The purpose of customer contact programmes is to help you deliver tailored information to your customers. One example is news of a special offer that is relevant to a past purchase — another is a reminder sent at the time of year when a customer traditionally places an order. Contact programmes are particularly useful for reactivating relationships with lapsed customers. Do your best to make sure that your customers feel the extra contact is relevant and beneficial to them — bombarding customers with unwanted calls or marketing material can be counter-productive. Newsletters and email bulletins allow you to keep in touch with useful information.

10

DEALING WITH THE CUSTOMER COMPLAINTS

It is a fact of business life that not all customers will be happy, even in the finest run businesses, problems, mistakes, or even bad luck can cause people to be dissatisfied with your products or service. When people are unhappy, they will often complain. Many businesses tend to try and ignore complaints, or pass them off as irrelevant, however, if dealt with well, they can actually provide your business with a strong advantage.

10.1. TYPES OF CUSTOMER COMPLAINTS

1. *Letters*: Letters are a very common form of complaint; they are generally seen as the most official way of complaining. This means that most customers will only use a letter of complaint where they feel there is a serious dissatisfaction, and where the business has a separate address for complaints or head office. Letters have an advantage to your business, as they allow you time to look at a problem, solve it, and reply to the customer; hopefully ensuring they are satisfied enough to remain a customer.

2. *Spoken Word to Employees*: The most common form of complaint, particularly in retail businesses; is face to face with an employee (usually the front line staff). This could take the form of a passing word or gesture, and can be for small or large problems. Typical comments include things such as: "This is not the first time...", "I can't believe that..." or even a 'tut' noise in a sentence. They are generally informal complaints or comments, only occasionally do they turn into full scale complaints. Although there is no official complaint in most cases, spoken word comments can provide information on the everyday problems that customers are experiencing, and provide an opportunity for your employees to solve these problems, both for these customers, and for future ones.
3. *Phone Calls*: These are another common form of complaint, generally used for informal minor complaints, but can also be used by a highly dissatisfied customer who does not wish to write. The frequency of phone complaints generally depends on how much your business uses the phone; a call centre will receive many more complaints than a basic office line. Phone complaints allow you to look into a problem, but do not usually give you as much time to solve it as a letter or email.
4. *Email*: Emails are similar to letters; however they tend to describe smaller problems that are expected to be solved in a much quicker time. The number of email complaints you receive will depend mostly on how widely you use email, and whether there is a specific enquiry or complaints email address.

10.2. IMPORTANCE OF RESPONDING TO CUSTOMERS COMPLAINTS

There are many reasons why you should listen to, and respond to your customers complaints; the following are some of the most important:

1. *Development*: The most important reason why you should listen to complaints is very simple. If someone is complaining, the chances are, there is a problem in your products or service that is causing it. Listening to complaints allows you to find out what the problems are with your business, and solve them. Solving problems may cost money; you may need to give refunds or replacements, but you will normally regain much more than this over time by retaining the customer. Fixing a problem once will help you keep the customer who made the complaint, but fixing it permanently will help keep all customers satisfied, and maybe even help to bring in some new customers.
2. *Loyalty*: It has been shown in several pieces of research that customers who complain, and have a problem solved are generally much more loyal than those who are simply happy with the business. If you can fix a complaint quickly, it shows not only that your business respects the customer and wishes to provide a good service; but also that you can be relied upon, even when things go wrong. It can provide a customer with a sense of security in your business, making them much less likely to go to your competitors.
3. *Lost Customers*: There is a basic choice with dissatisfied customers; Let them complain, and try to solve their problems; or watch them go to your competitors. Although there are few proven figures, most experts believe that you are up to 10 times

more likely to keep a complaining customer (whose problem you try to solve) than you are one who says nothing.

You should also remember that it costs up to five times as much to win a new customer than to keep an old one, even if keeping a dissatisfied customer costs you now, in the long run, it will almost certainly save you money. If a customer complains, it gives you a chance to make them satisfied with your business again, and for this reason, you should encourage dissatisfied customers to complain.

4. *Employees*: If a complaint is the result of a mistake by an employee, a complaint will help you to know where problems lie. Minor problems can be fixed by reminding employees of certain information or processes, major problems can be looked at over a period of time, with the aim of long term improvements. In repeated cases of employee fault, you should consider giving verbal warnings.

Front line employees can often bear the complaints caused by other employee's mistakes, but attempting to solve all problems revealed by complaints will help to keep your customers happy. Matters can also be helped if you give employees enough training and empowerment to deal with complaints and problems quickly.

A business that provides quality products or services is seeking complete customer satisfaction. In situations where customer complaints occur, the complaint must be dealt with immediately and the cause of the complaint rectified. Some companies are not concerned with quality and often ignore complaints or deal with them dishonestly.

When the customer pays for a product or service, it is assumed that the product will work correctly or that the service received is as promised. Ideally, the customer will be satisfied, and there will be no complaints. If there is a problem, and the customer complains about it, the company should quickly answer the complaint and solve the customer's problem. This is often done through the company's customer service activity. To make sure the customer is completely satisfied, some companies will provide some special service or a reduced price on another product. This is done to assure the customer will come back for more business.

When a company sells a product or a provides a service, part of the pricing should include the cost of servicing a certain percentage of defective products or complaints. The second thing a company should do upon receiving a complaint is to seek to rectify the problem. Although a company hopes not to get complaints, they often can be blessing in disguise.

Sometimes problems can be caught and fixed before they cause serious negative feedback or even legal problems. It is in the company's best interest to solve any problems and try to make sure that they don't happen again. Businesses that don't bother about satisfying their customers usually get more customer complaints. Answering them can, of course, cost the company money. Some companies will try to mollify angry customers but many don't even bother.

Have you ever experienced poor service or purchased a defective product and complained about it, only to have your complaints fall on deaf ears? Many companies that have plenty of business feel they don't need to bother with complainers. These businesses become very independent, especially if they have a product or service in demand. Some continue to succeed, even though they ignore customer complaints, but many will pay the price of lost business and degraded reputation in the long run.

A company that responds and apologises mollifies the complaining customer. But some of these companies never rectify the problem, like the hotel in the above story. The act of responding to the customer and apologising is good business. Not fixing the problem is risky, though, and may backfire on the company.

In today's litigation crazed society, the hotel would have been sued for millions. Perhaps that is not so bad, if it is a case of ignoring problems. But if it was an honest mistake, such litigation can be destructive to the business as well as to society. We all pay more for things, because businesses must insure themselves against nuisance lawsuits.

10.3. HOW TO SOLVE CUSTOMER COMPLAINTS

One of the best ways to help make unhappy customers feel better about your business is to listen. This shows that you care about your customers, and are looking out for them. Employees receiving complaints should always be friendly, polite, and helpful; and try their best to resolve the problem if they can. Even if a problem cannot be totally solved, the fact that your business did everything you could to help will make the customer feel much less negative about your business, hopefully enough to keep them with you.

Sometimes it can be difficult for an employee to feel like helping an angry customer, particularly if the problem is not their fault; however it is crucial that they remain polite and helpful at all times. Remember that body language is a large part of communication, so listening while looking away will just make the customer think you are ignoring them.

When a customer complains, you should always offer them a solution to the problem. If you cannot directly fix the problem, offer them something else to try and keep them satisfied. There are many different types of solution, but they could all turn a disappointed customer into a happy one:

1. *Replacement*: If you sell a product that has broken, offer a replacement. If an exact replacement is not available (or not wanted) you can try replacing with a similar make or model. A replacement solves any problem with the product, it may cost you the value of a new product, but losing the customer will probably cost much more in the long run.
2. *Refund*: If a customer is really unhappy with a product or service they may want a refund. This will mean a loss of the sale revenue, but providing a refund without hassle will strongly improve the chances of the customer returning again. In some cases a partial refund may solve minor problems.
3. *Fixing*: If there is a problem with a product, try fixing it! If a customer has a problem with your service, try taking steps to solve the problem and prevent it happening again. If the problem is an employee, speak with them, or if it continues, consider giving a verbal warning. If there is a common employee problem, you may be able to help solve it with training.
4. *Money off Next Purchase*: For smaller problems, it may be satisfactory for you to offer the customer money off of their next purchase with you. This helps to ensure that they will return to you, whilst minimising the cost of solving the problem.
5. *Apologise*: Sometimes one of the most effective forms of solution can be an apology, informally for minor problems, or written for major problems. An apology should be genuine, and may go alongside other forms of solution, particularly if the problem

is significant, or the customer is an important one. An apology shows that you care about the customer, and that you are aiming to put right any problems they have encountered.

10.4. HOW TO TURN CUSTOMER COMPLAINTS INTO MORE SALES

Customer complaints can cause you to lose future sales from customers and from everybody else who hears about their bad experience. Or you can turn customer complaints into more sales from these same customers and the people they influence. How you handle your customers' complaints determines which of these two results you get. Here are some simple actions you can take to turn customer complaints into more sales.

1. *Plan for Complaints*: You can never eliminate every customer complaint. Some mistakes happen regardless of how carefully you try to prevent them. Expect to get a few complaints periodically. It's part of operating a business. Handle complaints with a positive attitude. Strive to preserve your relationship with the complaining customer instead of your immediate profit from them. Make your customer happy now and they will reward you later with more sales.
2. *Make Resolving Complaints a Priority*: Surprise your customer with a quick response to their complaint. If you cannot solve the problem immediately, let them know you consider it a priority. Then do whatever you can to resolve the problem fast. The longer a customer has to worry about getting their problem solved the less likely they will accept a satisfactory solution and remain your customer.
3. *Conduct Yourself Professionally*: Conduct yourself professionally even when a complaining customer

does not. Complaining customers sometimes act hostile because they expect you to resist solving their problem. You can calm their hostility by letting them know you genuinely want to help them. Assure them you will do everything possible to solve their problem.

4. *Take Responsibility*: Take responsibility for resolving your customer's complaint even if the problem was not your fault. Apologise for the inconvenience. Briefly explain the probable cause of the problem. Then tell your customer exactly what you will do to correct it. Don't focus on blaming someone else for the problem. It sounds like an excuse. And never stretch the truth in your response to a complaint. Making excuses and explaining something the customer suspects is inaccurate can destroy your credibility.
5. *Compensate Your Customer for the Inconvenience*: Complaining customers hope they can get a satisfactory solution to their problem. But they often expect to get something less. Surprise them by solving their problem AND giving them something extra to compensate them for their inconvenience. This helps customers forget about the problem they had. Instead, they will remember the special attention you gave them.
6. *Follow Up to Confirm Satisfaction*: After solving your customer's problem, follow up to confirm their satisfaction with the outcome. This reinforces your relationship with the customer.
7. *Take Action to Prevent Similar Complaints*: After resolving a customer complaint, try to identify exactly what caused it. A complaint often reveals some weaknesses in your business procedure. Many times this weakness is minor and you can

easily correct it to avoid similar complaints in the future. Customer complaints can cause you to lose future sales from customers and from everybody else who listens to their sad story. Don't let that happen to you.

Use these simple actions to turn your customers' complaints into more sales.

10.5. HOW TO ENCOURAGE CUSTOMER COMPLAINTS

1. *Open Details*: The best way to encourage complaints and comments is to have open contact details. Include a contact address, phone number, and email address on all correspondence, allowing customers to contact you immediately and easily in the event of a problem. The quicker they can contact you, the quicker you can solve their problems.
2. *Friendly Staff*: Having friendly and helpful staff will encourage customers to talk about problems they are having with your business, helping to solve problems before they happen. Friendly staff will also help you to deal with complaints, listening to customers rather than trying to argue with them.
3. *Comment Slips*: Give customers the opportunity to tell you how they feel about your business. Provide them with comment slips or invite large customers to speak with you personally about how they feel about your business. On correspondence, state that you are open to contact on problems, e.g.: "If you have any problems, do not hesitate to contact us." If you invite comment, then people are more likely to respond, giving you a better look at the both the positive and negative areas of your business, and allowing you to deal with them as necessary.

SUGGESTED READINGS

Alessandra, Anthony J.; Wexler, Phillip S. *Non-Manipulative Selling*. Reston, VA. Prentice-Hall.

Anderson, R., Hair, J.; Bush, A. (1992). *Professional Sales Management*. McGraw-Hill. New York.

Black, Robert.; Jan Srygley-Mouton. (1970). *Guideposts for Effective Salesmanship*. Chicago: Playboy Press.

Bolton, Robert.; Dorothy Grover. *People Styles at Work*. New York: American Management Association.

Brescoli, James.; Dahm, Ralph M. (1995). *Opportunities in Sales*. Lincolnwood, IL: VGM Career Horizons.

Brooks, William T. *High Impact Selling*. New Jersey: Prentice-Hall.

____________ . Travisano, Thomas M. *You're Working Too Hard to Make the Sale!* Chicago: Irwin Professional Publishing.

Camenson, Blythe. (1997). *Real People Working in Sales and Marketing*. Lincolnwood, IL: VGM Career Horizons.

Carew, Jack. *You'll Never Get No for an Answer*. New York: Simon & Schuster.

Goldstucker, Jac L.; Jose R. de la Torre, Jr. (1972). *International Marketing*. Chicago: American Marketing Association.

Herold, Jean. (1988). *Marketing and Sales Management: An Information Sourcebook*. Phoenix, AZ: Oryx.

Miller, Robert B.; Heiman, Stephen E. *Strategic Selling*. New York: William Morrow and Company, Inc.

Montgomery, Robert L. (1981). *Listening Made Easy*. New York: Amacom.

Morgan, Bradley J. (1993). *Marketing and Sales Directory*. Washington, D.C.: Visible Ink.

Petersen, Glen S. *High-Impact Sales Force Automation*. Florida: St. Lucie Press.

Reilly, Thomas P. *Customer Service Is More Than a Department: It's an Attitude*. St. Louis: Motivation Press.

____________. *How to Sell and Manage in Tough Times and Tough Markets*. St. Louis: Motivation Press.

____________. *Selling Smart!*. St. Louis: Motivation Press.

____________. *Value-Added Selling*. New York: McGraw-Hill.

Sinetar, Marsha. (1987). *Do What You Love and the Money Will Follow*. New York: Dell Publishing.

Treacy, Michael.; Wiersema, Fred. *The Discipline of Market Leaders*. Addison-Wesley Publishing Company.